A Philosophy of Cultural Scenes in Art and Popular Culture

This book seeks to understand culture through the lens of scenes, analyzing them aesthetically and culturally as well as understanding them through the frameworks of gender, social networks, and artworlds.

It is common to talk about the cultural and intellectual scenes of early twentieth-century Vienna, the visual art scene of postwar New York, and the music and fashion scene of the swinging London. We often think about artists and works of art as essentially belonging to a certain scene. Scenes might offer a new approach to study what is possible, what is a tradition, and/or to discuss what are the relevant units of contemporary culture for research. The book posits that scenes explain a lot about how the artworld and the cultural field function. Vivienne Westwood, Rene Magritte, Roman Jakobson, Arthur C. Danto, Susan Sontag, James Baldwin, and Didier Eribon are among the figures included in the book, which examines scenes in cities such as Moscow, Bombay, New York, London, Paris, Brussels, Helsinki, and Bratislava.

The book will be of interest to scholars working in art history, cultural studies, philosophy, film, literature, and urban studies.

Max Ryynänen is Principal Lecturer of Theory of Visual Culture at Aalto University.

Jozef Kovalčik is lecturer of Aesthetics at Comenius University in Bratislava, Slovakia and director of Slovak Arts Council.

Routledge Focus on Art History and Visual Studies

Routledge Focus on Art History and Visual Studies presents short-form books on varied topics within the fields of art history and visual studies.

For more information about this series, please visit: https://www.routledge.com/Routledge-Focus-on-Art-History-and-Visual-Studies/book-series/FOCUSAH

A Philosophy of Cultural Scenes in Art and Popular Culture

Max Ryynänen and Jozef Kovalčik

Routledge
Taylor & Francis Group

NEW YORK AND LONDON

First published 2024
by Routledge
605 Third Avenue, New York, NY 10158

and by Routledge
4 Park Square, Milton Park, Abingdon, Oxon, OX14 4RN

Routledge is an imprint of the Taylor & Francis Group, an informa business

Library of Congress Cataloging-in-Publication Data
Names: Ryynänen, Max, author. | Kovalčik, Jozef, author.
Title: A philosophy of cultural scenes in art and popular culture / Max
Ryynänen, Jozef Kovalčik.
Description: New York, NY : Routledge, 2024. | Includes bibliographical
references and index. |
Identifiers: LCCN 2023025786 | ISBN 9781032536101 (hardback) |
ISBN 9781032536125 (paperback) | ISBN 9781003412786 (ebook)
Subjects: LCSH: Culture—Philosophy. | Arts and society. |
Artists—Social networks.
Classification: LCC HM621 .R99 2024 | DDC 306.01—dc23/eng/20230615
LC record available at https://lccn.loc.gov/2023025786

ISBN: 9781032536101 (hbk)
ISBN: 9781032536125 (pbk)
ISBN: 9781003412786 (ebk)

DOI: 10.4324/9781003412786

Typeset in Times New Roman
by codeMantra

Contents

Introduction

In Woody Allen's *Small Time Crooks* (2000), Ray (played by Allen himself) and Frenchy (Tracey Ullman) establish a cookie shop with their "colleagues." The bakery is, though, just a façade for another enterprise. From the basement of the tiny business space, they dig a tunnel into the neighboring bank with their friends. The heist fails, but the bakery, originally intended to be a "smoke screen," becomes a hit, and in the end a franchise.[1]

Ray and Frenchy, originally poor and desperate, become filthy rich. They buy incredible luxury items. In their new job as corporate managers, they meet new (kinds of) people. Once they accidentally hear their dinner guests mocking their lack of "taste." The pressure to acquire that becomes so unbearable that Frenchy takes the initiative to hire a mentor, David (Hugh Grant).

David takes Ray and Frenchy to museums and contemporary dance performances, i.e. he presents them to the New York art scene. But there is more to it. One could say that he presents them the bourgeois part of it. He also teaches the misfits wine and fancy upper-class (mainly French) eating habits – but in the end he is revealed to be quite a crook himself too.

Allen uses this part of the film as a comical attack against petty bourgeois values and the way art and design is, in certain circles, used (as Hannah Arendt would call it) in a "philistine" way, for "self-civilization."[2] In those circles, one is really nothing if one does not have "good taste." Even more, of course, neither should one forget the way class differences become marked and reinforced through this practice. This latter perspective is well known for most of us through Pierre Bourdieu's pioneering studies on the French middle- and upper-class, and their art-consuming habits. In *Distinction: A Social Critique of the Judgement of Taste* (1986),[3] one finds plenty of notes about the status-hungry bourgeois, their standards, and ways of appropriating art. Many scholars have since walked especially in Bourdieu's footsteps and studied these phenomena, which have an economically and societally supportive role for the artworld.[4]

When the art scene is portrayed in cinema, the focus is often on the bourgeois side, where works of art are status symbols. But although, for example, we have worked in art and design for 20 years, we do not have much personal

DOI: 10.4324/9781003412786-1

experience of the "financial sector" of art, nor bourgeois life. Of course, it flourishes in cities like London or New York, where rich people invest in "culture" – and, naturally, for example, France, together with the Netherlands, has a long, even founding tradition of this type of bourgeois use of art and design as cultural capital. It is just that in the art scene one can live and work without any contact with this world. Many artists work and aim to sell art to the upper class, even only to the nouveau riche, for sure. But often bourgeois interests in art do not resonate with the aspirations artists have. Even many artists who aim to sell feel uncomfortable when they have to meet their collectors and buyers. The impact of this system has still, of course, been central in the development of the art system. One could not imagine what the artworld would look like without the Dutch painting market that was boosted in the seventeenth century, and it might even be that what people have been calling kitsch in art could at least partly echo this connection, as something that this "steering group" of buyers has desired and in a way "ordered," although straight orders are not typical of the modern or contemporary artworld.[5]

And, of course, every major art scene has its own Burgtheater – a city theater for the bourgeois, that, for example, the Austrian author Thomas Bernhard mocks in his ironic books – and shiny galleries selling clean-cut fetish objects for home decoration, seen as cheesy by the societal end of the art scene, but still having the aura of "authentic art." Still, this reality does not touch much upon the everyday of the political part of the art scene, which thrives on manifestations, panel discussions, and "artivist" acts. Neither does one, from these two, always find that much of a strong connection to the nearly technocratic communities of new media and robot-driven art, where collaborations with engineers and computer scientists dominate. In addition, poetry slams and underground publishers are often as far from art commerce as they are from the hardcover book sales and award-driven sectors of the book market. This is what scenes are about. Scenes, as we shall argue in this book, are often quite autonomous entities that are able to support different atmospheres, tastes, and (even) aesthetics, and they are often very diverse.

They share certain traits, though. A person who enters a cultural scene for the first time notices that it is in many respects very different from other territories of society. It has its own written and unwritten rules, structures, and agents that other scenes might share (but not always), keyholders and gatekeepers, winners and losers, the extraordinary and the average, without forgetting the key figures of the scenes who everyone knows – loving or hating them. In the same way, there are not just downshifters from the middle class in the scenes, but also people with really rich and really poor backgrounds. The more one turns toward the experimental and the alternative, the more one finds people who are refugees, working class, or just otherwise marginalized in society. The commonly known story of the art market and its people with upper-class or middle-class backgrounds and "taste" talks only, really, only about one part of the scenes, as art scenes in the end, in our experience, are less restricted class-wise, and yes, we have, not coming from the middle-class ourselves, really kept our eyes open in this respect.

Art scenes are geo-cultural platforms where artists, their admirers, followers and critics, dealers, curators, intellectuals, and scholars meet – with diverse educations, social backgrounds, traditions, and ambitions. Some "inhabitants" of art scenes are extremely liberal. There are not as many distinctions between class, race, sexuality, health, and gender as in most other areas of life – gallery keepers in Mumbai shout out loud "no caste" – but, of course, everything is relative, and the art scene is no paradise. One thing is clear: to some extent, anyone entering the scene has to leave behind them their cultural background and accept the unwritten rules and expectations, sensitivities, and atmospheres that prevail.

The art scene is a very special kind of territory which consists of official and commercial institutions, but also alternative ones that are so strong that they could be sometimes considered to be central for the scene.[6] Of course, there are some exceptions, for example, operas or classical music orchestras whose contact with "independent" agents could be described as weak or non-existent. Official institutions are often, though, very much dependent on the acceptance of the more alternative sides of the scene, and even their content comes, with time, in the end often from the alternative scenes that fill up museums 10 or 20 years after their blooming in shadier venues. Alternative artistic entities are respected, and they strongly determine the character of particular art scenes.

Economically, everyday living in the art scene is quite wide-ranging. The same person who is starving on Monday is offered a fancy dinner in a Michelin restaurant on Tuesday by a curator and cocktails on the roof of a museum on Thursday by the museum director. Some even famous artists and curators live in underworld bunkers. These broke people fly around the world sharing their critical ideas about not just society but the very institutions that pay their bills. They are invited by Ivy League universities to give (embarrassingly often pro bono) talks. They sip champagne without paying for it but they are only able to make as much money as cleaners. There is a lot of free work done in the art scene, and/but, if one has "made it" career-wise, there are many gray economies around that are not visible in taxation. One receives food, drinks, books, travel, theater tickets, and free use of exhibition or rehearsal spaces as payment.

Some of the cultural capital of the French bourgeois that Pierre Bourdieu wrote about in his *Distinction* (1986) is worth nothing in most parts of the art scene: Monet's waterlilies, major museum exhibitions (with their inflatable Picassos in the museum shop), and standards of "quality" and "taste" are a bad joke in reality where people would rather discuss the interesting sound the broken electric door of the corner shop makes. A friend of ours did not in the end enter a major museum in Berlin, as there was a piece of paper being blown around by the wind outside of it, which was much more interesting. He stayed outside, filming it. The scene lives its own life in peculiar ways.

Jack Halberstam has written in his *In A Queer Time and Place: Transgender Bodies, Subcultural Lives* (2005) about the way the world of the queers has a different rhythm and human geography following its traditions of night life, for example, the way people mostly do not have children and the way the whole culture echoes the counterculture and forced outlaw nature it still inhabited a couple of decades ago (and still does in many countries). Halberstam also writes that, for example, addicts and/or "junkies" are in the same situation – not able or willing to follow mainstream paths of modern life.[7] One could also write about art scenes through this perspective. Of course, to begin with, artists are relatively often queer. One aspect of the artworld is the strong presence of sexual margins, and the presence of their culture might even have had an impact on the development of the culture of many scenes. The culture of the scenes really offers a strong alternative to other ways of life through its very specific nature. For example, a plumber, a salesman, or an office employee do not have anything resulting from their jobs that would resemble openings or premiers. An active and unique social life comes naturally with the arts. In an "art time and place," people hang out and join extravagant events, which begin mostly, at least in our scenes, at six or seven in the evening. It is no news that the art and popular culture scenes are pioneers in contemporary lifestyles that one could tag as liberal (even if there are some exceptions), "creative," and/or just laid-back, although there are many more open clashes and experimentalism in the art scene than in the clearly more middle-class hipster culture, where clashes are not wanted at all, to not break the pleasant flux of the downshifting middle-class lifestyle.[8]

Most of us do not have a mentor when we enter the artworld, like Ray and Frenchie had in Woody Allen's film. A bourgeois background might help a bit, sometimes, but only in some parts of the scene. The toolkit received from middle-class parents with its dusty respect for all classical music and its Sunday museum-shopping practice, without forgetting the active reading of books nominated for national book prizes, will not work as good currency in the professional scene if not framed the right way. In alternative galleries and experimental music studios, the bourgeois end of the art scenes is not often even seen to be part of the scene. It does not truly even work the same way socially. People hang out less, and their way of life is less different from mainstream culture. On the other hand, the presence of the bourgeoisie can be strong. It can even define the specific character of a scene. Allen's movie zooms in to a scene like this.

People who are experienced still often need mentors for adapting to unknown scenes, though. Artists, curators, museum directors, producers, and scholars of art work hard to accommodate visitors and new colleagues. Friends in Mumbai send us to an opening at the Clark House Initiative "which we must see," where the crowd keeps explaining where to head next – without forgetting that people in scenes where we land often give us books and pamphlets on the local work. "You have to visit Leopold, the café," they might tell us (still in Mumbai) – but in Jyväskylä, Finland, everyone knows that in the end one always lands in the Vakiopaine bar. Local friends call us when they need help to host visitors (this one goes to Helsinki): "It would be great if she could meet you when she comes. Like you, she is very much into bio art. Can you take her to the Bio Art Society? After that, let's meet in Corona."

Still, to get back to studying the very basics that scenes share, it is not hard to remember, coming from a working-class/less-privileged background, what it meant when the evenings were suddenly full of invitations to openings with colleagues and peers, and how the sharing economy inside of the arts was overwhelming and inclusive right from the first day of being a legitimate member of a scene – and how travel, free fancy dinners, and drinks became commonplace. For those who are not from a privileged background even alternative art scenes might feel luxurious. If we would write a scene memoir, this could be a meaningful starting point. Being a member of an art scene is not just about aesthetics and art, nor is it just about professional issues and institutional frames. It is very much also about just a different conception of time like is noted with certain schedules for openings and performances. In the art scenes, there are "tribal codes," from dressing to body gestures, that mark belonging, and they are readable only by those who, often without realizing it, are insiders.

Entering an art scene is, for someone arriving from science or economy, for example, like arriving on a close but at the same time distant planet. Now, someone could say all territories of life and work are different, and it takes time to get in. But art scenes are different in a different way. Like skateboarders and intellectuals in major cities, the people of the art and popular culture scenes have something additional to profession and just "networks." Scenes are not just about production, consumption, and distribution of artworks. They are much more the shared territory – the place of things happening and making sense. They are like villages where people live. They are safety nets. They are also places where meanings, interpretations, and new experiences start taking place.

"Members" of scenes face both difference and familiarity when they change scene – whether they change from one subscene to another one (e.g. from the visual art scene to the music scene) or relocate to another city with a scene (while not all cities, especially small ones, have scenes). There are hidden paradigms, meanings, boundaries, and values. Most of the time, a person who changes scene feels lost in the language games, nuances, sophisticated, and often ironic commentaries when a conversation about artworks begins. Soon, though, the meta-level of understanding scenes helps and makes everything easy again, as there is anyway also a shared coding, and a cluster of ways of interpreting, evaluating, and experiencing which helps to solve site-specific codes. Together scenes make up global artworlds, some actively, some rather passively or marginally. And they can be very different.

Art galleries in Tokyo have already seen all boundaries crossed, so do not think of shocking the crowd. The Cairo scene has long been a hotbed of video art, which has set certain standards for the moving image. Following, e.g. the magnified presence of poet and creative writing teacher Mamta Sagar, Bengaluru's literature scene shares a victorious history of and maybe even a pressure for multilinguistic practice and teaching. And Wuppertal still lies under the shadow of choreographer Pina Bausch, who made the small town world-famous as the home of the biggest name in contemporary dance chore-ography for her most active years of practice.

Some people are connected to scenes because their parents or relatives belong to them. Some come from "nearby," from families where commercial creative work sustains a living, or where the appreciation of the arts has made the family follow closely what happens in the scene. These people need to defend their membership less, because they know how the system works at least a bit. It is typical of scenes that there are characters who are talked about as sons or daughters of someone, who don't really do anything, but are around, and are accepted, right from their possible first professional experimentations.

Most people still really have to work to get in. And people need to relocate. A great book on this is Patti Smith's *Just Kids* (2010). The book focuses on the endless passion to find a way to get to New York, the place where things happen, and where there is "freedom." It is full of descriptions of scenes that are typical of New York, like the "psychedelic atmosphere" of the area around St. Mark's Place, the community that lived at the Hotel Chelsea at the time, and the leather-clad gay and drag queen scene that was a radical visual part of the spirit of the city in the 1970s.[9] And people keep popping up in Tel Aviv, Buenos Aires, and Jakarta, searching for not just more freedom, which is always a very relative issue, but an alternative life style, compan-ions, new friends, places where to perform, and connections that could help in career-building.

Even whole scenes can relocate, when a country that used to be free sud-denly turns too totalitarian to support free culture – or when closed coun-tries open their borders. The way artists that had been harassed in their home countries (in Africa and South America) found a new home in the suburbs of Stockholm in the 1970s and the relocation of Yugoslavian experimental artists to Vienna in the 1960s and 1970s and later in the 1990s during the Yugoslav Wars are examples of scene migration. In the latter case, there were so many people moving from Yugoslavia to Vienna that the Yugoslavian scene became a scene inside of the grand Vienna scene. In the former case, the shattered remains of other scenes formed a new immigrant art scene, a subscene of the broader Stockholm cultural scene.

Scenes can die in various ways, and not just following politics and relocations. *Hell: The History of Norwegian Black Metal* (2020)[10] tells the tale of the radical metal music scene in Norway in the late 1980s and early 1990s, a story of a network of metal enthusiasts with roots in various cities and the main joint, the shop Helvete (Hell) as their home base in Oslo. What first comes together slowly through the exchange of demo tapes, sparse concerts, copy machine printed fanzines, and a group of people hanging around Helvete burns down fast together with the churches (about 50 attempted arsons between 1992 and 1996, some successful, the most famous being Fantoft Stave Church, lit by Burzum singer Varg Vikernes, who was though not the only church-destroyer of the scene), the suicide of Dead (singer of Mayhem), and the sad murder case of singer Euronymus (by, again Vikernes). A short, intensive period, which made black metal less technical (virtuosic technique was a typical trait of death metal), increasingly raw, punkish, in a way, and dread-driven, decayed fast, leaving space for a more mainstream conception of the same musical drive.

Art and popular culture scenes can grow very autonomous. But there are other scenes, too. There are intellectual scenes, also famous ones, from early twentieth-century Vienna to Paris. There can also be chess scenes or scenes for people who are into Japanese youth culture, if they are a group big enough. There are feminist and queer culture scenes – Berlin and New York are famous – and there are cities without scenes.

Michaela Pfadenhauer nails the problematic of "post-traditional" communities. She frames them as life-worlds.[11] Life-world ethnography has often been used for studying youth scenes. The focus on style- and theme-specific phenomena has made the approach valuable in efforts to understand youth. John Irwin's pioneering work on the concept of the scene is also the basis for Pfadenhauer's work.

[T]he label [scene] indicates that these worlds are expressive – that is, people participate in them for direct rather than future gratification – that they are voluntary, and that they are available to the public. In addition, the theatrical metaphor of the word "scene" reflects an emergent urban psychological orientation – that of a person as "actor", self-consciously presenting him – or herself in front of audiences[.][12]

Marc Augé writes, "In the modern place people of various ages and origins meet and find a kind of aesthetic alibi for their presence together in the clash or juxtaposition of styles."[13] Without forgetting how much these lifestyles and scenes as everyday culture (of, e.g. fashion) can have impact on the production of culture, this is still not the point of what we are seeking to discuss here. Of course, what is meant, for example, by a rock scene is not just the gigs and the recordings, but a whole lifestyle with bars, clubs, and other places where people meet – without forgetting clothes and even shared food tastes – and these places leave a mark on artistic production too.

It is important to note that although scenes have been studied by ethnographers and scholars in cultural studies, there is not much to be drawn from their work if one wants to understand the impact of scenes aesthetically or intellectually. Scholarly work on music scenes discusses topics like "the country music scene," referring to large chunks of people connected only partly by geo-cultural wholes and even more through record sales and music media.[14] Dana Nell Maher's brilliant work on the Sacramento poetry scene[15] is on art, and reading it is eye-opening, but still, it is only about the invisible glue and the multifaceted shared spaces and the mindset and the social practices that scenes are about. What we are interested in, where, of course, our forerunners help us a bit, but still not much, is the way scenes are relatively autonomous cultural entities with a lot of capacity to constitute their own cultural realms and sustain culture, and the sources for what art can be and how things can be viewed aesthetically. The way some scenes have their own aesthetic, and how they sometimes produce genres and waves of culture in a remarkably distinguished way, is the miracle we chase to understand and explain. In one's first week in Berlin, one already learns what art in Berlin means – and 20 years ago a couple of nights clubbing in Manchester was enough to wake the tourist up to understand that there was "something very different going on here." After the first week in Mumbai – in whatever part of the cultural scene – one easily has a bunch of playful and skillfully executed small craft books published by some underground press in one's suitcase. And after a month in Havana, most people return finally understanding the complex rhythm of, for example, son music, which has played in the background night and day, enough to reveal its secrets. After that, more contemporary musical acts of the Latin music scenes start making sense – even for a Finn.

Will Straw writes,

> Scene is a term which flourishes within everyday talk about urban cultures but which, until recently, was marginal within academic writing on cities. Journalists, tourists and city-dwellers will speak of the Temple Bar scene in Dublin, the techno music scene in Berlin or the new hotel bar scene in Montreal, but the scale and character of the phenomena being referred to will fluctuate with each usage. Scene designates particular clusters of social and cultural activity without specifying the nature of the boundaries which circumscribe them. Scenes may be distinguished according to their location (as in Montreal's St. Laurent scene), the genre of cultural production which gives them coherence (a musical style, for example, as in references to the electroclash scene) or the loosely defined social activity around which they take shape (as with urban outdoor chess-playing scenes).[16]

It is true that scene is also a concept used for not just cultural scenes in a location (which is our interest), but that one can discuss, for example, the world of country music, its distribution, and communities, but this way of using the term has not much in common with the way scenes come together geographically in cities with plenty of culture. Scene used in the non-geographical way is actually just a perspective on what, for example, country music is today. Why even call it a scene? Even more, the studies in culture done so far have no interest in scenes as constitutive cultural worlds. The way certain things are culturally possible because of a scene and the way scenes can help us to see things differently from an aesthetic point of view is what we are after – although we could also be interested in, for instance, the outdoor chess-playing scenes mentioned by Straw and sometimes just the loose character of urban areas where people dress in certain ways. Our main interest is, though, to dive into the magic of cultural production, the places and practices, communities, and platforms that build us as *homo aestheticus*, and the so far quite invisible artistic (here referring to both art and popular culture) impact of scenes. Rather than discussing the history of music in the Netherlands, we'd be for having a book about the Amsterdam jazz scene – or, rather than reading about the history of music in Germany, we'd be happy reading a book about the history of music in West Berlin. Iain Chambers shows beautifully in his *Popular Culture: The Metropolitan Experience* (1986), how cities, cityscapes, urban meeting places, and urban relocations build, disrupt, distribute, and connect cultures, and although Chambers does not explicitly discuss scenes, his work has here been really inspiring the writing of this book.[17] A thankful note should also be sent to Greil Marcus and Henry Parland's essays on urban culture. Here and there, one finds notes on differences between scenes, although not really through a thorough analysis of their local nature. Howard S. Becker mentions the different working conditions of writers in the US and Russia[18] and comes close to scene thinking.

Chapter 1, "Three Giants: Vivienne Westwood, Roman Jakobson, and René Magritte, and their Vertical and Horizontal Travels through the Scenes," tells the story of three prominent artists and intellectuals, focusing on the scenes and lack of scenes their professional history brings forth. It is in our interest to show how changing the scene is a major issue in the life of both artists and intellectuals, and how they can contribute to their formation. Three exceptional careers introduce us to the topic of scenes in a concrete way. Our example professionals with a high impact on arts, culture, and academia change class (Westwood), city (Magritte, Jakobson), and scenes both vertically and horizontally (from down to up for Westwood, but horizontal movement for, e.g. Jakobson) in ways that show us the importance and meaning of scenes.

Chapter 2, "Sketching Out the Structure of Scenes," is our attempt at describing all kinds of stereotypes, patterns, and anomalies that construct the world of cultural and intellectual scenes. We start by asking where scenes start in Western culture – and we go through basic taxonomies in an introductory way. What do scenes consist of? What kinds of agents are typical for cultural scenes? What is needed for a flourishing scene? There is no recipe for a scene, but there are some types of support that make things happen. What are the inherent logics of scenes? When looking at different scenes, different types – from the design scene of Milan to the musical scene of Manchester, or the contemporary art scene of Vienna – what is there to learn?

Chapter 3, "The Scene-Driven Art Theories of Danto and Sontag – and the Urban Thinking of the Twentieth-Century Philosophers," sheds light on the presence of scenes in the work of two classics from the 1960s, Arthur C. Danto and Susan Sontag, and continues then to take a look at the philosophers of urban culture of early and mid-modernity (Baudelaire, Benjamin). In the former case, the notes that Danto and Sontag have made about contemporary culture are actually partly about a scene, and even if both authors, with their respective texts on the artworld and camp, have global appeal and meaning, it does not hurt to see how their works are site-specific, too. In the latter case, we notice that the history of philosophy of urban culture has not been aiming for universal knowledge as much as we have thought, for example, in the case of Baudelaire and Benjamin, who are often quoted for their notes on flaneurs and street culture, for instance. It looks like at least some classical notes made about cities in philosophy are site-specific, even scene-driven.

Chapter 4, "If Beale Street Could Talk like Greenwich Village: Scenes, Class, Ethnicity and Contemporary Urban Studies," deals with the power relations of scenes, and the power relations between scenes and the life beyond them (e.g. working-class life) – and the way these societally vertical exchanges work. It dives in, again through two examples, shorter in breadth, though, to discuss center and periphery, wealth, and poverty. James Baldwin's geographically tiny step from Harlem/The Bronx to Greenwich Village tells us a lot about class, ethnicity, and scenes. The change of scenes made sense for the young writer – who also traveled to a far-away scene, a geopolitically and geoculturally very different Istanbul, to find his way further. Didier Eribon's existential travel from working-class life in Reims to the cream of the intellectual scene in Paris, where he deliberately forgot his background, and his memory-filled, literary journey back in *Returning to Reims* (2009) show not just the way upper-class scenes can make us forget lower-class scenes. The story also surveys the lack of scene that sometimes, but only sometimes, haunts the modern working class and its urban areas.

Chapter 5, "Aesthetics of the Scenes," is the key chapter for understanding art and popular culture scenes. As we have already laid bare the many structures and currents in scenes, this chapter aesthetically theorizes scenes as constitutive of culture, autonomic to a great extent. How to grab the issue? What can really be said? Could scenes overshadow nations in the future as the geographical framework of art and cultural history? In what sense are scenes constitutive aesthetically and/or artistically and/or intellectually?

In Chapter 6, "Film Scenes: Professionals, Institutionally Homeless Filmmakers, and Film Enthusiasts," we use the last slot of the book to sketch out what film scenes are, to include one example of a case study in the book. How do film scenes differ from other cultural scenes? We take a look at the studio system, which dominated film scenes for a long time. We also discuss the role of film clubs, the way being a critic is one way to become a director in film, and the connections that the film scene has to other art scenes – i.e. all the peculiarities, which make film scenes different.

Notes

1 We wish to thank Tyrus Miller, Giacomo Bottà, Paco Barragán, Sezgin Boynik, Yuriko Saito, Zoltan Somhegyi, Erol Mintaş, Davide Giovanzana, Matti Tainio, Adam Andrzejewski, Riikka Perälä, Jani Sund, Antti Rannisto, and the anonymous referees of Routledge for their valuable comments on our ideas. We also want to draw the reader's attention to Minna Henriksson's inspiring drawings on the dynamics of the contemporary art scenes of Helsinki, Istanbul, Zagreb, Ljubljana, and Belgrade. Minna Henriksson, *Maps 2005–2009* (Ljubljana: R-tisk, 2011). The book is partly based on the ideas developed for our article "The Art Scenes," *Contemporary Aesthetics* 16 (2018), https://contempaesthetics.org/newvolume/pages/article.php?articleID=847, which we also refer to in some chapters.
2 Hannah Arendt, "The Crisis of Culture?" in *Between Past and Future* (New York: The Viking Press, 1961), 197–241.
3 Pierre Bourdieu, *Distinction* (London: Routledge, 1984).
4 See, e.g. Jarkko Pyysiäinen and Max Ryynänen, "Downgrading with Style: Middle-Class Role Anxiety and the Aesthetic Performance of Role Distance," *Poetics* 172 (February 2019): 43–53.
5 See Paco Barragán and Max Ryynänen, "Kitsch: From Rejection to Acceptance – On The Changing Meaning of Kitsch in Today's Cultural Production," in Max Ryynänen and Paco Barragán, eds, *The Changing Meaning of Kitsch* (New York: Palgrave, 2023), 1–62.
6 See Jozef Kovalcik and Max Ryynänen, "Margins of Aesthetics," *Contemporary Aesthetics* 14 (2016): https://contempaesthetics.org/newvolume/pages/article.php?articleID=744.
7 Jack Halberstam, *In a Queer Time and Place: Transgender Bodies, Subcultural Lives* (New York: New York University Press, 2005). See especially the first chapter.
8 For notes on hipsters and aesthetics, see Lenka Lee, "New Beauty: Between Hipsters and Folklore," *Popular Inquiry* 2 (2019): 43–52.
9 Patti Smith, *Just Kids* (New York: Eco, 2010).
10 *Hell: The History of Norwegian Black Metal* (*Helvete: Historien om Norsk Black Metal*). Mini-series. 2 h 52 min. Directed by Thomas Alkärr and Håvard Bråthen. NRK1. Norway.
11 Michaela Pfadenhauer, "Ethnography of Scenes. Towards a Sociological Life-World Analysis of (Post-Traditional) Community-building," *Forum: Qualitative Social Research*. 6, no. 3 (September 2005): 43.
12 John Irwin, *Scenes* (Beverly Hills: Sage, 1977), 23.
13 Marc Augé, "Paris and the Ethnography of the Contemporary World," in *Parisian Fields*, edited by Michael Sheringham (London: Reaktion Books, 1996), 175–179.
14 For an overview, see, e.g. Giacomo Bottà, *Deindustrialization and Popular Music: Punk and 'Post-Punk' in Manchester, Düsseldorf, Torino and Tampere* (Lanham MD: Rowman and Littlefield, 2020).

15 Dana Nell Maher, *The Sociology of Scenes, the Sacramento Poetry Scene* (Las Vegas NV: UNLV Theses, 2009). https://digitalscholarship.unlv.edu/cgi/viewcontent.cgi? article=2125&context=thesesdissertations.
16 Will Straw, "Cultural Scenes," *Loisir et Société / Society and Leisure* 27, no. 3 (2004): 411–422. Quote on page 412.
17 Iain Chambers, *Popular Culture: The Metropolitan Experience* (Essex: Methuen, 1986).
18 Howard S. Becker, *Art Worlds* (Berkeley, Los Angeles, and London: University of California Press, 1984), 5, 6. Becker's work is also just sociological. He is interested in all professional and logistic aspects of artworlds (division of labor, p. 7), not their aesthetic (p. xi).

Bibliography

Alkärr, Thomas, and Håvard Bråthen, directors. *Hell: The History of Norwegian Black Metal* (*Helvete: Historien om Norsk Black Metal*). NRK1, 2020. Mini-series. 2: 52.

Arendt, Hannah. *Between Past and Future*. New York: Penguin Books, 1961.

Augé, Marc. "Paris and the Ethnography of the Contemporary World." In *Parisian Fields*, edited by Michael Sheringham, 175–179. London: Reaktion Books, 1996.

Becker, Howard S. *Art Worlds*. Berkeley, Los Angeles, and London: University of California Press, 1984.

Bottà, Giacomo. *Deindustrialization and Popular Music: Punk and 'Post-Punk' in Manchester, Dusseldorf, Torino and Tampere*. Lanham MD: Rowman and Littlefield, 2020.

Bourdieu, Pierre. *Distinction*. Translated by Richard Nice. London: Routledge, 1984.

Chambers, Iain. *Popular Culture: The Metropolitan Experience*. Essex: Methuen, 1986.

Halberstam, Jack. *In a Queer Time and Place: Transgender Bodies, Subcultural Lives*. New York: New York University Press, 2005.

Henriksson, Minna. *Maps 2005–2009*. Ljubljana: R-tisk, 2011.

Irwin, John. *Scenes*. Beverly Hills CA: Sage, 1977.

Kovalcik, Jozef, and Max Ryynänen. "Margins of Aesthetics." *Contemporary Aesthetics* 14 (2016). https://contempaesthetics.org/newvolume/pages/article. php?articleID=744.

Kovalcik, Jozef, and Max Ryynänen. "The Art Scenes." *Contemporary Aesthetics* 16 (2018). Https://contempaesthetics.org/newvolume/pages/article.php?articleID=847.

Lee, Lenka. "New Beauty: Between Hipsters and Folklore." *Popular Inquiry* 2 (2019), 43–52.

Maher, Dana Nell. *The Sociology of Scenes, the Sacramento Poetry Scene*. Las Vegas NV: UNLV Theses, 2009.

Pfadenhauer, Michaela. "Ethnography of Scenes: Towards a Sociological Life-World Analysis of (Post-Traditional) Community-building." *Forum: Qualitative Social Research* 6, No. 3 Art 43 (Sep 2005).

Pyysiäinen, Jarkko, and Ryynänen Max. "Downgrading with Style: Middle-Class Role Anxiety and the Aesthetics Performance of Role Distance." *Poetics* 172 (February 2019): 43–53.

Smith, Patti. *Just Kids*. New York: Eco, 2010.

Straw, Will. "Cultural Scenes." *Loisir et Société / Society and Leisure* 27, No. 3 (2004): 411–422.

1 Three Giants

Vivienne Westwood, Roman Jakobson, and René Magritte, and Their Vertical and Horizontal Travels Through Scenes

Arriving at scenes, traveling from one scene to another, and leaving scenes: these are typical moments when the word scene arises in art writing. When someone is already in the midst of his/her career, like Picasso in Montmartre, there is not much talk about scene, partly, of course, due to the fact that at least big artists have, at this point, had a role in building the scenes they occupy. So, the context no longer poses any challenges, clashes, or even always visible stimulations, as much as it does when someone enters it.

We have chosen three different stories to paint, with broad brushstrokes, a preliminary idea of what scenes are, starting with movement between scenes that show their importance and effect. The stories of fashion designers Vivienne Westwood and Roman Jakobson exemplify movement between scenes in a way that could lay out a heuristic base for further investigations.

Westwood, who started from true poverty and ended up in the highest position possible (star, professor) in the fashion world, shows in a fantastic way, how the arrival at the right scene at the right moment can be crucial. The movement which through Westwood's designer work became known as punk was bubbling under in London in a way that made it a small but increasingly visible scene at the time of her early success. It shows how great artists both need a certain kind of scene to get it going, but also fuel the scenes where they work.

In Jakobson's case, we witness how a Russian immigrant, through an incredible amount of energy, lands in different places from Prague to New York and forms communities, and perhaps whole scenes or important components for building scenes, around him, that are still visible, in our academic surroundings (e.g. through the work of Noam Chomsky and Claude Levi-Strauss). The original scene is, of course, important here. Jakobson fueled the birth of structuralism that landed neatly in the world of art, but it is worth remembering that he started in the Moscow art scene, where linguistics and art had an important and fruitful companionship through the growing formalist movement.

Rene Magritte, our third example, perfectly demonstrates the mobility between center and periphery, between two different scenes, one in his native

DOI: 10.4324/9781003412786-2

Belgium, and the other in Paris, the capital of art in Magritte's prime. He had to fight for recognition in Paris, where he never really felt at home, and the scars from this battle are still visible in his art. Magritte cannot be understood without understanding the role of the change of scenes during his career.

Vivienne Westwood: Recycled Chrome Tops from the Salt and Pepper on the Christmas Tree

> Everything that has happened subsequently for me: London, Manchester, Malcolm [McLaren], fashion, art and politics, I can date to 1958. I was nearly seventeen, and everything in my world changed. My mother and father decided we children would have a better chance in life if we moved to London and they bought a post office in Harrow. (…) (W)hen we came down to London, (…) I applied for Harrow Art School (…) and I got in.[1]

Fashion designer Vivienne Westwood's (1941–2022) story of her arrival on a powerful and challenging scene is just one out of many, although the narratives usually feature an adult who often knows what s/he wants, not a teenager. In the case of one of the most famous fashion designers ever, the move meant a major change in the surrounding community and its glass ceilings.

Career advice in Westwood's native home of rural Chesire (North West England) was "especially for (…) girls" not very encouraging, thinking about art and culture. Westwood's friend who wanted to become an architect was told she must become a hairdresser "because she was artistic." There's nothing wrong with this content-wise, as we might personally be even more interested in hairdressing than architecture (and we lament the lack of a philosophy of hairdressing), but the comment is more about class difference and gender paradigms than an aesthetic enthusiasm for hairstyles. Another classmate who wanted to become a journalist was told by the headmaster that she had "wildly unrealistic" plans, and then was "told to be a nurse. (…) I came from a place where you didn't have this visual language."[2]

At this early stage of Westwood's career, London (at the time, *the* center for arts in Europe) opened up a whole new world, where there were more options for the future. She enrolled in the Harrow Art School (today's University of Westminster), where she found dress design. If her childhood was about "recycled chrome tops from the salt and pepper as Christmas tree decorations," she did not forget her class background; after one year on a jewelry and silversmith course she quit, saying "I didn't know how a working-class girl like me could possibly make a living in the art world". She had to work on something else. But she had found fashion.[3]

How this evolved into a fresh out of the oven practice in the pre-punk 430 King's Road shop SEX (1974-1976) run by Malcolm McLaren (the manager of the Sex Pistols), where addicts and prostitutes hung out, where Westwood earned her "street credibility,"[4] and how the trashy King's Road sales tables launched a career in *haute couture* fashion, is one of the most amazing vertical moves in the history of artistic careers. It is not that the community which started the provocative punk rock movement and fashion would not have had contact with the avant-garde – Westwood claims that Guy Debord's 1967 Situationist International book *The Society of Spectacle* would have been *the* foundational book of the early punk movement[5] – nor that they would not have been educated, but as punk was really a mix of art school-inspired rebels and working-class youth (people from the *Lumpenproletariat*), the way her dresses are cat-walked in Paris and Milan today remind us that her career was anything but typical. Westwood, who was once responsible for the look of the Sex Pistols,[6] is as much high society as anyone can be. Her clothes fill the wardrobes of oil millionaires and Hollywood stars, and the same forms and idea rhizomes make it in totally different spheres. Punk was a completely new scene and a global subculture that in the aforementioned period gained its visual form, but as it became "art history", its original scene – Camden (nothing more than a small area in London) somehow became overshadowed and forgotten, and like the once detested Baroque or Rococo, it became just another "style."

Subcultures, it's good to note, can have a key role in some scenes, such as the London punk scene, which we can see as a subculture at least in the beginning. Reading Dick Hebdige's classic *Subculture* (1979) where differing forms of non-mainstream cultures are discussed, one is quickly reminded of how subcultures have a stronger role in some cities while in others they are not important. For example, in London subculture is really the thing, and it has been like that for a long time. Hebdige's classical work suggests that living in and belonging to any subculture is more of a lifestyle project, but, of course, subcultures also affect the production and consumption of culture, albeit rarely as the key for an entire city's cultural scene, which is always multi-faceted, not only in terms of class and age, but in terms of the various practices that inhabit it.[7] Still, it is somehow interesting and paradoxical to think that a subculture can dominate a city for a while.

When one thinks of vertical movement between scenes, it is hard to find anything as illustrative as Westwood's case. She ran her first shop Nostalgia of Mud 1982–1983, rocked Italy and Paris throughout the 1980s, taught at the Angewandte (University of Applied Arts Vienna) in Vienna at the turn of the 1990s,[8] and rose to true global stardom at the turn of the millennium. Making activism commonplace in fashion, she actually took it from lowbrow to highbrow, as it had been a part of her practice even before SEX.

The vertical movement here is something to learn from, starting with the reasons and needs to change scene and practice (e.g. economy) to the way the same practices have a different impact on different levels of cultural production and media coverage. Interestingly, Westwood brought some of the artistic practices and styles from the lowbrow fashion scene and made them commonplace in what could be called more highbrow. Her collections, like *Savages* (1981), *Worlds End* (1983), and *Clint Eastwood* (1984-1985, and even *Punkature* (1982), that were presented both on the scenes of London and in Paris, were often street credible and highlighted phenomena that were typical for experimental outsiders to the markets and the professional fashion scene.

Although the rich affect the poor and the people with power affect those without, the tale of the marginal and the poor that took their culture to the world of the powerful is a romantic one. That´s why poverty and marginalization, as starting points for careers that boom through all levels of society, have, of course, always been at the heart of scene narratives. Legend has it that in 1966 Julia Kristeva arrived in Paris from Bulgaria at the age of 25 with 5 dollars in her pocket – "armed with a doctoral fellowship and a small suitcase."[9] Shusaku Arakawa came to "New York with nothing but a few dollar bills and the telephone number of Marcel Duchamp in his pocket."[10] Patti Smith arrived in the same city with "nothing."[11] And, to rewind historically, Franz Jozeph Haydn arrived in Vienna "without a coin in his pocket, and with only poverty staring him in the face."[12]

The difference in the stories of 'business geniuses who arrived in America with nothing and made a fortune' such as Jerry Yang (founder of Yahoo), Indra Nooyi (CEO of PepsiCo) and Andy Grove (co-founder of Intel Corporation) – and artists, is that stories about artists and scholars do not in the end focus that much on money and gaining a place in the spotlights of society or media, but about how they became important for their scene (at least first). The stories, though, tell a lot about the scenes that supported their growth, development, and work. The celebrated artists are described as bringing new ideas to the scene, but even then, the scene has to be ready for it, and this is something that these stories nail too. Not any arrival in any place would make a story.

In many narratives, the person's immigrant or underdog status is accentuated. The list of migratory art legends could be extended to Yayoi Kusama (New York), Milan Kundera (Paris), and Marcel Duchamp (New York). Arriving at scenes is, of course, part of the history of immigration, but in these stories, it is often not just about survival, but making it in art too in a new context, and it is often something that is restricted only to metropolises.

Stories about arrivals at scenes in art and scholarship are often about turning points. Westwood's story is about class, gender, and an era when a scene turned wild. She rode its gigantic waves to global stardom. If Sonya Delaunay might have painted *con sordino* for a while, to be, possibly voluntarily, in the shadow of her (less talented, we think) husband Robert Delaunay (to not compete with him in the same market), and joined the fashion forces, starting with interior decoration and ending up working with clothes (Jean-Paul Gaultier homaged her work in the 1980s and 1990s),[13] working-class Westwood abandoned dreams about contemporary art due to the sheer impossibility to make enough money from it, as she did not have a wealthy background. And what is interesting in her case is the creative output in the lower side of the scale, which then, like a readymade package, traveled up to new scenes vertically and changed the highbrow of fashion. The trashy objects that were once King's Cross material were transformed into haute couture. The artist moved from the raunchier, more improvised lowbrow scene of her city's broader cultural scene and became famous in the professional fashion scene. But before that she needed to change from the contemporary art scene, that she had just accessed, to the fashion scene, where she found herself.

Roman Osipovich Jakobson: The Voracious Reader

I [Noam Chomsky] arrived at Harvard in 1951, after a couple of years of graduate work in linguistics, feeling quite confident that I knew my way about the field. One of the first things I did, naturally, was go to see Roman Jakobson, who was of course a legendary figure. Our first meeting was rather curious – we disagreed about everything imaginable, and became very good friends. (…) At the very time, he had created an intellectual milieu in Cambridge that had very powerful attraction and that I found myself quickly drawn into, as were many others of that academic generation. Out of this ferment and debate, in which Roman was always a central, even though sometimes an absent figure, quite a few ideas were formed and developed – many of them his, others bearing his imprint – which have had a significant impact on the development of linguistics and cognitive psychology, and fields that I know nothing about, in the following years.[14]

It seemed that Jakobson was good at creating and sustaining communities, and, we'd like to think (or at least ask) about the scenes around him (milieus, in Chomsky's words). It says something that during his lifetime he was a member of something like 30 learned societies.[15]

If Vivienne Westwood offers us a perfect narrative for understanding vertical mobility, and so also illuminates class difference and the center vs. the periphery polarization of different scenes (one should, of course, not forget that she initially moved from the contemporary art scene to the fashion scene within London's broader scene), the career of Roman Osipovich Jakobson (1896–1982) shows us how very different scenes (like art and linguistics/semiotics) in the same location can intertwine and how one person can be a key figure in establishing and/or developing many different scenes.

The history of structuralism reckons the story of this giant of theoretical thinking, who changed the life of not just the formalists, but also Umberto Eco, Noam Chomsky, Jaques Derrida, and Claude Levi-Strauss, right from the beginning, as one which developed in a melting point of humanities an art. "During the 1920s the Moscow and Petersburg groups suffered a theoretical and collective diaspora," as Richard Bradford writes[16] and in Jakobson's case the mobility between the scenes became essential.

Jakobson was born in Moscow. He became interested in folktales at a very young age, and "by the time he was six, (he) was already a "voracious reader.""[17]

> He learned French and German when he was very young and discovered the poetry of Pushkin and Verlaine and then Mallarmé when he was only twelve! In 1912, he joined the new and particularly creative futurists, and read the poetry of Velimir Khlebnikov and then that of Vladimir Mayakovski, with whom he became friends, as he did with the painter Cazimir Malevich.[18]

Jakobson entered the historical-philological faculty at the University of Moscow in 1914, and a year later, at the age of 19, he "founded the *Moskovskij Lingvistiĉeskij Kruzok*, the Moscow Linguistic Circle", with six other students,[19] which expressed the aspiration to study linguistics, poetics, metrics, and folklore.

Together with its Petersburg counterpart OPOJAZ, with which Jakobson was closely involved, the Moscow Circle became the founding moment in what has become the largest interdisciplinary growth industry of twentieth-century academe, variously known as critical theory, semiotics, structuralism, literary linguistics, cultural studies...[20]

One of Jakobson's aims was to defend the Russian avant-garde, to which he himself also belonged, not just as a thinker, but as a poet, as, at an early age, he had already met major artistic figures such as Marinetti and Mayakovsky.

> The academic years 1912-1913 and 1913-1914 were for me years of literary and scholarly maturation. (Since those times I've become accustomed to think in the framework of academic years.) In those years it seemed absolutely clear that we were experiencing a period of cataclysms in the visual arts, in poetry, and in science, or rather, in the sciences. It was then that I heard the lectures of a young physicist who had just returned from Germany and was reporting on Einstein's first work on the theory of relativity; this was still before the general theory of relativity. On the other hand, my impressions of French artists alternated with those of the emerging Russian painting, which was partly abstract and then became totally abstract.[21]

Jakobson's academic and artistic surroundings were special from the start, while he was studying Slavic Languages in Moscow University. For most linguists, the artistic surroundings wouldn't make sense to take up in a discussion about lifework, but in Jakobson's case, the artistic milieu made a difference. Russian avant-garde poetry had taken radical routes and the same could be said about Russian modernism, not to mention formalism. "I grew up among painters, and the fundamental questions of space, color and the contours and texture of paintings were as familiar to me as the fundamental questions of the verbal mass in poetry as compared to usual speech."[22] Jakobson assisted Vladimir Mayakovsky, the great revolutionary poet, at young age, as he was excellent in languages, and his tight literary network had already developed during the early days of his career.

The art scene in Moscow, his point of departure, was very linguistic (or semiotic, one could say), if one thinks about futurists and formalists. And this is what he exported to Czechoslovakia in the 1920s and the 1930s. He visited the country on a Red Cross mission two years after the forming of that country, officially aspiring to take care of prisoners of war (being the interpreter of his group), and moved to continue his doctoral studies. In the 1930s, he was docent and later professor at the Masaryk University in Brno, where his colleagues were suspicious about him.[23] Besides political reasons, there were scholarly ones. Jakobson defended Russian formalism against traditional nationalistic approaches.[24] He became, as fluently as in Moscow, one of the founders and the leading figure of the Prague Linguistic Circle, which lasted from 1926 to the Second World War, and which actually was in some sense a twin scene, consisting of the academic life mainly in Prague but also Brno, and hosted many émigré intellectuals from Russia, besides Jakobson, Petr Bogatyrev, and to a certain extent Nikolaj Trubetskoy.[25] This group fostered the intellectual development of René Wellek and Jan Mukařovsky and many other Czech, Ukrainian, Russian, and German scholars; most notably, giants of philosophy such as Husserl and Carnap visited the circle and engaged in dialogue with its members.[26] Looking at functional elements in language and turning that into a question of functional elements in art and culture was something which had been founded collectively in the Moscow scene, but which in Prague was raised to new heights, and then led to the birth of French structuralism (thanks to the meeting of Jacobson and Claude Levi-Strauss in New York), together with the Italian variants of semiotic thinking (Umberto Eco at the forefront). It is not farfetched to guess that at least some of Jakobson's ideas on how linguistics could explain art must have come from the way linguistics and arts were connected in his scene, similar to the way that dance and tech or painting and music can be closely connected.

"I grew up in a milieu of painters," Jakobson said.[27] "Thus, it can be said that the formalists and futurists (…) were essentially responsible for this push in the direction of linguistics."[28] The Prague circle took the name of structuralism because of its interest in structures, which were like an ensemble moving culture, the fundament for cultural action.[29] Jakobson ultimately became one of the founding members of the Linguistic Circle of New York. Wherever

Jakobson could be found, a circle was formed, which had a huge impact on culture and scholarly work.[30]

He was a true cosmopolitan, "at home in Moscow and Prague and Brno and Copenhagen and Oslo and Uppsala and New York and La Jolla and Ossabaw Island and Peacham, Vermont, and Cambridge"[31] not to mention Paris, where Jakobson never lived, but continually visited.[32] Looking at his life history and reading the tales of his colleagues, he seemed to have been shepherding and intellectually feeding flocks all around the European and the American East Coast academic world. Still, you could always see the traces of the original scene where artists and linguists were connected. This model of a wandering academic (Jew) is not, of course, his "invention". One could think of Moses Maimonides's travels (Spain, Morocco, Egypt) or the way the Frankfurt School did not just emigrate to teach (Frankfurt, New York, California) but also brought with themselves the remains of an entire German critical philosophical scene when they came to the US – like the (also) Jewish composers, who left Germany and brought their craft for classical music to Hollywood. It is just that the case of Jakobson shows one person's effect on a variety of intellectual scenes, and his authorlike presence at many sites.

Michel Foucault's 1969 "What is an author?"[33] poses a set of questions to open up the at a time troubled mess of the idea of the author in early 'postmodernist' France. Answering Roland Barthes's discourse on losing the 'person' in artistic work (to dive into the tradition and formal play of text) and the need to get rid of the "intentional fallacies" of art research[34] through an analysis of the ways that authorship has become an issue in late European civilization, Foucault claims that we should note the way Marx and Freud are in some sense "authors" of Marxism and Freudianism.[35] To a certain extent, opening new ways of thinking leaves the trace of an "author" but Jakobsonism is not a key word even in linguistic studies. Still, when one looks at his travels from Moscow to Prague, and then to New York, and the impact he had, one can ask: was Jakobson the author of the Prague semiotic scene or the New York linguistic one – or is this saying too much, even if we thought that he would have been only one of the authors, a co-author, so to speak? What could it mean that a scene has an author – or a couple of them? Breton could be said to be in at least some way the author of surrealism. Of course, it is not as simple as naming someone the author of a book, but in the same way, sometimes scenes would not really develop or at least not develop to become what they ultimately became without certain key figures.

Family names such as *Bitter, Chitter, Ditter, Fitter, Gitter, Hitter, Jitter, Litter, Mitter, Pitter, Ritter, Sitter, Titter, Witter, Zitter* all occur in New York. Whatever the origin of the names and their bearers, each of the vocables is used in the English of New Yorkers without colliding their linguistic habits. You had never heard anything about the gentleman introduced to you at a New York party. "Mr. Ditter", says your host. You try to grasp and retain this message. As an English-speaking person you, unaware of the operation, easily divide the continuous soundflow into a definite number of successive units.[36]

This take on the 'name scene' of New York is Jakobson at his best. One can imagine him walking in, with a bottle of vodka in his hand (he was a notorious alcoholic), and immediately grasping what this 'scene' was about, what codes were used, and which morphologies existed. Being able to build and inspire scenes in new places is, of course, also about sensitivity to the existing ones, an ability to grasp how the local scene functions, without forgetting that one must arrive with something very good in the suitcase to have an impact. And Jakobson did. He franchised the Moscow art and linguistics scene.

This enthusiasm must have helped Jakobson drag people into his circles, that eventually, we interpret, were lighting up whole scenes. Looking back on discussions with Jakobson, Chomsky writes:

> I was never actually a student of Roman's, technically speaking, but my own thinking was very much influenced by his work, and in other ways, too, he had a significant influence on my personal life. In fact, it's very unlikely that I would have stayed in the field at all if it hadn't been for his interest and encouragement, which at the time was quite unusual among professional linguists. And this was all the more unusual, because he really didn't agree with what I was doing, and he thought it was probably not on the right track.[37]

René Magritte: The Treachery of Scenes

In September 1927, René Magritte arrived in Paris from Belgium, which the Parisian surrealists considered to be a regional and bourgeois place (both might have been true notions on the city's culture). He had taken part in the Belgian surrealist movement, but also, though gaining a name, did not find his way to the top of the business, as Brussels was too regional[38] – which is interesting: he is not the only one who did not find his fame in his original scene, but had to change to another one to become recognized. It is not just that bigger scenes make artists impactful, but that many famous artists haven't found appreciation in smaller scenes, and so had to leave for bigger (often more radical) ones to achieve it. In Paris, where Magritte spent only 3 years, staying in suburban Paris, just as he had stayed in suburban Brussels, not becoming a snob of the center,[39] he became a part of a scene inside a scene, the large group of surrealists in the incredibly large Parisian art scene (where painters and poets shared a lot).

> Magritte knew that he needed to move to Paris, the heart of the Surrealist movement, to get noticed. He (...) soon met important Surrealists like Max Ernst, Salvador Dali [who arrived the same month] and Joan Miró.[40]

The movement, which at first accentuated more techniques and methods such as automatic writing, was turning its gaze toward dreamlike scenarios. Led by writers, its focus was not in images. Magritte, who never gave up his Walloon accent or bourgeois "respectability" (he also did not choose to live in Bohemian quarters but in the bourgeois suburbs of Paris, which was outrageous for an artist)[41] was treated arrogantly and snobbishly by the Parisian intellectuals who were running the movement. "In Paris, accent was not a trivial matter. Bad French smacked of bad manners," as Alex Danhev, the author of *Magritte: A Life* (2020) notes.[42]

It got to the point that when Breton wrote his treatise on painting and surrealism in February 1928, *Le Surréalisme et la peinture,*[43] he "forgot" to even mention Magritte, despite the fact that Magritte had quickly carved out a space of his own in the community. Magritte also understood that he had to study Hegel to get into the thinking which defined the surrealist movement. Theory was a key into the smaller scene of the surrealists, although it was not a must everywhere on the Parisian art scene at the time.

The surrealist manifests are full of paradoxes, but they are all not just for fun. Georges Bataille commented that the surrealists had a manic relationship to dialectics. Like politicians and statesmen who had been obsessed with Hegel's dialectical philosophy throughout the nineteenth century, there was a growing wave of Hegelianism in early twentieth-century France (which really hit the philosophical scene through key thinkers such as Jean Hippolyte a bit later). One of its first breeding grounds was the Surrealist movement.

In 1924, the movement was launched by poets who had converted to Hegelianism. Hegel, who was a development-centered thinker, placed music and poetry on a higher level than visual arts in his philosophical system. In brief, the development of the human spirit had moved from the east to the west, and after religion, first the arts, and then philosophy held the central position in the development of human culture.[44]

One can think that it was quite natural that visual arts did not win the pole position in Hegel's system, as painting and sculpture were nothing compared to poetry and literature in the early nineteenth-century German-speaking world. (We do not use the word scene here, as urban development might not have been on that stage there, and art had spread out everywhere in the country, in upper class circles, with philosophy.) But one can also ask if the Hegelian success of poetry was about an affinity with philosophy. Even Hegel himself was sometimes quite poetic, but even more, German philosophy was a hotbed of poetic philosophers such as Novalis and Herder, and Hegel was announcing the death of art.

This is not to say that art wouldn't give an expression of the spirit's understanding of itself. It differs from philosophy and religion by expressing the spirit's self-understanding, not in pure concepts or in images of faith, but in and through objects that have been specifically made for this purpose by human beings. Such objects, conjured out of stone, wood, color, sound, or words, render the freedom of the spirit visible or audible to an audience. Art allows us to contemplate and enjoy sensual images of our own spiritual freedom. This is the reason for their beauty. Art exists because we need a distinctively sensual form of human self-expression and self-understanding.

Dialectics is the most influential of all of Hegel's thoughts. Though it isn't always that dominant in his writing, the passages he created pushed Marx to write his philosophy and Pierre-Joseph Proudhon to pen his radical ideas on what he called (and coined) anarchism. Hegel's dialectic philosophy, which Marx famously turned up and down in his political thinking, was based upon at the time fresh ideas on the development of human consciousness and human self-realization. Hegel saw world history as the story of human development, or, to be more precise, a story of the development of something he called the Spirit (*Geist*), and it is in this developmental process, where the high season of art was over.

Hegel's dialectics, his way of framing philosophically (in a speculative manner) human and societal development, was based upon the idea of oppositions loaded with potential. To understand the construction, one has to first imagine a historical phenomenon. Talking about major changes one has to then, of course, think of phenomena which dominate in culture and society. In Marx's reading of Hegel, this is, quite naturally, capitalism, the sort of industrial revolution which he and Engels had witnessed both in Germany and England. The thesis (the name of this force) – the unfair treatment of workers and the proletarians, already includes and even produces a negation, which is to abolish its own reign. It feeds the rise and growth of an anti-thesis. In Marx's reading, this means that the poorly treated people gain class-consciousness and turn their political energy against the system and the dominant forces. By dividing society and not offering a decent living for the lower classes, capitalism so forges its own end. Through the clash and the revolution, culture and society sublates (*Aufhebung*) onto a new plane, into something that Hegel calls synthesis, a higher and better form of life. The clash is to be both destroyed and somehow preserved, followed by this more developed process and stage of culture and society (for Marx this part of dialectics meant communism). To become someone in his new scene, Magritte studied Hegel during his holidays. This memory turned into a painting in the late 1950s. In *Les vacances de Hegel* (1958), "Hegel on his holiday," Hegel no longer had the energy to work dialectically on a thing and its opposite, to sublate the opposition of thesis and anti-thesis. A glass of water simply remains on an umbrella and nothing happens.

Here dialectics does not reach synthesis, which is also the famous case of the Frankfurt School, which viewed twentieth-century dialectics as being only negative, no revolution arriving as a culture industry, mostly kitschy mass culture and kitschy high culture – not avant-garde or pure entertainment – would glue the negative whole together.

This is, of course, something Magritte did not know about, and the surrealists were all the more into expressing their Hegelianism through oppositions; in Magritte's case, visual oppositions, and the Frankfurters were only starting their career at the time. But like Zeno with his paradoxes, the Surrealists were into clashes and thought of these "paradoxes" as a sort of method and model for art.

In an even more famous painting from 1929, Magritte made Hegel visible in another way according to Didier Ottinger's *Nom d'une pipe! ou Comment Magritte rêva d'expédier Les vacances de Hegel* (2007).[45] Magritte painted a pipe.

The pipe in the picture, where the text is saying that this is not a pipe, is a neutral and quite realist pipe, leaning toward comics actually, or, well, it is not a pipe, but the image of a pipe – a thought which has become visible.

The painting is called *La trahison des images* (The Treachery of Images), and one must now remember that 1929 (two years after the arrival of Magritte, who had already been betrayed by Breton's book of Surrealist painting) was the most Hegelian period of surrealism. The painting is nowadays high-washed, but originally it was also popular culture, and appeared to the public as the cover of the Belgian *Variétés* magazine on 15 January of the same year.

Michel Foucault famously made the painting out to be a problem of semiology, a linguistic one so to speak – and we know that Foucault and Magritte were even in dialogue at one point. Of course, this is not a pipe, it is the image of a pipe – and this we know from various different interpretations and appropriations of the work. And Magritte was not against this reading. He said: "Of course it is not a pipe, just try to put tobacco in it."

But maybe the pipe is an act of allegiance and maybe even a critique of Breton's Hegelianism? This is what Ottinger neatly asks by recounting the Surrealists' Hegel debates and Magritte's overshadowed role at the time.

(According to Ottinger) *La Trahison des images* comments on a passage written by Hegel for the Phenomenology of the Spirit, where he discusses a piece of paper. The original passage discusses the way ordinary language often remains distanced, abstract, and too universal to grab the sensuality of our experience. In poetry, "paper" can again, through poetic writing, gain sensuality, and at the same time be an abstraction and sensually more present than everyday language (or even our real encounter with a paper, which is often not that conscious or sensual).

But why change paper into a pipe? At the time, Surrealism was aggressively fighting for power in the Paris art scene. Breton, together with Paul Eluard, wrote a parody about Paul Valery's poetry. Valery had written aphorisms about poetry, some quite kitschy. For example, he said that a poem should be the feast of the intellect – which Breton and Eluard twisted into "failure of the intellect" (or disaster). When Valery said that poetry was survival, Breton and Eluard mocked him: "poetry is a pipe."

The pipe must have been a big joke in the community, and everybody certainly knew how the word was used. Painting here exclaims its status as art. Painting is not poetry (pipe). But Magritte himself said that a painter's thoughts manifest themselves as images, and he was fighting for his position in an old debate.

In a letter to André Bosmans, written on December 5, 1963, Magritte wrote: "An image is not an expression of a thought, it is a thought."[46] And this thought is the invisible trace of the Parisian surrealist scene in the paintings that we often view as visual language games only. It could also be read as revenge against a scene that treated Magritte badly – so badly, that after four years, he retreated to his bourgeois Belgium (he really accentuated his bourgeoisness, maybe as an act of rebellion against the leftist artists of Paris). Looking at Magritte's paintings, not that much happened visually as a result of his move to the center of the artworld (at the time), but the texts, and this Hegelian trait is definitely what the scene made him do. The famous Magritte paintings echo the theory readings of the scene where they were painted, more than most of us have realized. The quiet strangeness of his early works gained another layer, through encountering hostile poets and philosophical discourse. The wordplay paintings testify to the strength of the presence of theory in art scenes. And, the complex code of the work was an attempt to work both artistically and theoretically to defend painting.

After the ignorance of the Parisian surrealist scene had made him unhappy, Magritte left for good[47] and assumed the role of "king of the Belgians," as Alex Danhev writes. "He represented an antipode to Paris and metropolitan hegemony,"[48] and so tells us a lot about the negative side of big scenes, and their power-relations. Paris might, of course, be a very special scene in this sense, as not all big scenes are arrogant – but making it wherever there is competition also means that not only pleasant things will happen to an artist.

Besides his mobility between two urban scenes, Magritte, bringing his weird stuff from Belgium, where it was not appreciated, to Paris, where it found a home, especially after a layer of local theory landed on it, shows how artists are in need of good scenes. Art has always been site-specific, of course. Looking at the green of Tintoretto (who never left Venice), like Venetian emerald waters, and Carpaccio's red paintings that must have fantastically suited the urban (often Carpaccioesque red) townscape of their time, one can ask how much might have been lost when their paintings were spread out in the Louvre and other museums far from their original 'home'. But here we clash with the historical necessity of not naming anything a scene. Quattrocento Florence might have had some scene-like properties, but still, a part of what scenes are is their post-community nature, the urban, free nature, where different meeting places from cafes to clubs make up a world that is socially as well as artistically fertile. They work like any network, community, and/or extended network/community, by building borders and trashing (often imagined) enemies.

Conclusion

Looking at these different stories, we can already see the structural issues connected to scenes, the vertical and horizontal movement between scenes, the arrivals at different scenes, and the reasons why people might leave a scene – and, for example, the way scenes sometimes crave adaptation from the artists who enter them.

Even more importantly, scenes are different, and the stories of people working out their careers through scenes are so diverse and their number so vast, that an interesting scene reader could easily be written and/or collected. It is also important to take a concrete look at how scenes are and can be viewed, and what kind of issues can be at stake in different careers and scenes.

But how much have scenes become theorized? There are not really any distinguished attempts to do that in terms of aesthetics or art theory (some works in anthropology come close, but not in any helpful way), but some classical works in aesthetics and cultural philosophy give us hints about how we can theorize scenes, and ultimately are at least a bit about scenes.

Notes

1 Vivienne Westwood and Ian Kelly, *Vivienne Westwood* (London: Picador, 2014), 72.
2 Westwood and Kelly, *Vivienne Westwood*, 69.
3 Westwood and Kelly *Vivienne Westwood*, 49, 77.
4 Westwood and Kelly *Vivienne Westwood*, 104.
5 McLaren even claimed to have met Debord, which probably was not true. Westwood and Kelly, *Vivienne Westwood*, 121.
6 Westwood and Kelly, *Vivienne Westwood*, 186.
7 Dick Hebdige, *Subculture: The Meaning of Style* (London and New York: Routledge, 1979).
8 Westwood and Kelly, *Vivienne Westwood*, 255, 323.
9 Anne-Marie Smith, *Julia Kristeva: Speaking the Unspeakable* (London: Pluto Press, 1988), 2.
10 Michael Whittle, "The Mechanism of Meaning: The Diagrammatic Genius of Arakawa and Gins," *Diagrammatology: Diagrams in Art and Culture* (blog). 20.4.2017. https://www.michael-whittle.com/diagrammatology/the-mechanism-of-meaning-the-diagrammatic-genius-of-arakawa-and-gins.
11 John Trimbur, *The Call to Write* (Boston MA: Cengage Learning, 2013), 228; later corrected to "a few dollars".
12 Cuthbert J. Hadden, *Haydn* (J.M. Dent & Company: 1902), 2. Project Guttenberg. https://www.gutenberg.org/files/3788/3788-h/3788-h.htm.
13 One reason for Delaunay's work in design was also due to her interest in applying modernist principles to everyday life. See, e.g. Whitney Chadwick, *Women, Art, and Society* (London: Thames & Hudson, 1990), e.g. 261–262.
14 Walter de Gruyter, *A Tribute to Roman Jakobson 1896-1982* (Berlin/New York: de Gruyter, 1983), 81.
15 Roman Jakobson, *My Futurist Years*, Compiled and Edited by Bengt Jangfeldt and Stephen Rudy (New York: Marsilio Publishers, 1997), see Introduction, ix.
16 Richard Bradford, *Roman Jakobson: Life, Language, Art* (London/New York: Routledge, 1994), 2.

17 Francois Dosse, *History of Structuralism. Volume I: The Rising Sign 1945-1966* (Minneapolis and London: The University of Minnesota Press, 1997), 5.

18 Dosse, *History of Structuralism*, 53.

19 Bradford, *Roman Jakobson*, 1.

20 Ibid.

21 Jakobson, *My Futurist Years*, 3.

22 Roman Jakobson & Krystyna Promorska, *Dialogues* (Cambridge MA: MIT Press, 1988), 6, 7.

23 Jindřich Toman, Příběh jednoho moderního projektu (Prague: Karolinum, 2011), 108. Toman draws attention to the dispute over whether Jacobson was sent to Czechoslovakia as a spy working for the Soviet Union.

24 See Tomáš Glanc, *"Jakobsonuv formalism 1935,"* in *Roman Jakobson. Formalistická škola a dnešní literárni věda ruská,* edited by Glanc Tomáš (Prague: Academia, 2005), 126–128.

25 See Jana Siren's excellent study on the role of structuralism in the artistic milieu of Czechoslovakia in the 20th century: Jana Siren, *On Imbricate Relations: Between Children's Books Visuality and the Structuralist Moment in East-Central Europe From the 1910s to 1960s* (Espoo: Aalto University, Master's Thesis, 2022). https://aaltodoc.aalto.fi/handle/123456789/115365.

26 See, e.g. Toman, *Příběh jednoho moderního projektu,* 141–142.

27 Dosse, *History of Structuralism*, 53.

28 Ibid. 54. Saussure became important only later, when Jakobson came upon the *CCL* in 1920, in Prague.

29 Ibid. 55.

30 Zavacká Marína's article "Dobrodruzstva akademickej mobility: Roman Jakobson na Slovensku", in English "Adventures in Academic Mobility: Roman Jakobson in Slovakia" (Marina 2018) nails the issue. "Academic mobility" should or could be a more studied phenomenon, as much as artistic mobility, as so many things happen through it. See Marína Zavacká, "Dobrodružstvá akademickej mobility: Roman Jakobson na Slovensku," *Historický časopis* (January 2018): 107–132.

31 Linda R. Waugh in de Gruyter, *A Tribute to Roman Jakobson,* 64.

32 Dosse, *History of Structuralism,* 53.

33 Michel Foucault, "Qu'est-ce qu'un auteur?" *Bulletin de la Societe francaise de philosophie* 63e, no. 3, 73–104.

34 Roland Barthes, "The Death of the Author," in *Image – Music – Text* (London: Fontana Press, 1977), 142–148; see also W.K. Wimsatt and M.C. Beardsley, "The Intentional Fallacy," *The Sewanee Review* 54, no. 3 (Jul – Sep 1946): 468–488.

35 Foucault, "Qu'est-ce qu'un auteur?".

36 Roman Jakobson & Moris Halle, *Fundamentals of Language* (Berlin & New York: Mouton de Gruyter, 1956), 1.

37 Chomsky's part in de Gruyer, *A Tribute to Roman Jakobson,* 82.

38 Alex Danhev, *Magritte: A Life* (New York: Pantheon Books, 2020), 153.

39 Danhev, *Magritte,* xxvi-xxvii, 154.

40 *Scholastic Art,* December 2013/January 2014, 6-7. For the broader story, see Danhev, *Magritte: A Life.*

41 Danhev, *Magritte,* xxix, 154. See also Philip Hensher's text for the *Spectator,* "The Life of Rene Magritte Was Even More Surprising Than His Art": https://www.spectator.co.uk/article/the-life-of-ren-magritte-was-even-more-surprising-than-his-art.

42 Danhev, *Magritte,* 182.

43 André Breton, *Le Surréalisme et la peinture* (Paris: Éditions Gallimard, 1965).

44 See, e.g. G.W.F. Hegel, *Aesthetics: Lectures on Fine Art,* Volume II (Oxford: Clarendon Press, 1975).

45 Didier Ottinger, *Nom d'une pipe! ou Comment Magritte rêva d'expédier Hegel en vacances* (Paris: L'Échoppe, 2007). Danhev recalls this story also in Danhev, *Magritte,* 189.

46 Ottinger, *Nom d'une pipe! ou Comment Magritte rêva d'expédier Hegel en vacances.*
47 Danhev, *Magritte*, 194, 195.
48 Danhev, *Magritte*, xxix.

Bibliography

Bradford, Richard. *Roman Jakobson: Life, Language, Art.* London and New York: Routledge, 1994.

Barthes, Roland. "The Death of the Author." In *Image – Music – Text.* Translated by Stephen Heat. London: Fontana Press, 1977.

Breton, André. *Le Surréalisme et la peinture.* Paris: Éditions Gallimard, 1965.

Chadwick, Whitney. *Women, Art, and Society.* London: Thames & Hudson, 1990.

Danhev, Alex. *Magritte: A Life.* New York: Pantheon Books, 2020.

de Gruyter, Walter. *A Tribute to Roman Jakobson 1896-1982.* Berlin and New York: de Gruyter, 1983.

Dosse, François. *History of Surrealism, Volume I: The Rising Sign 1945-1966.* Translated by Deborah Glassman. Minneapolis and London: The University of Minnesota Press, 1997.

Foucault, Michel. "Qu'est-ce qu'un auteur?" *Bulletin de la Societe francaise de philosophie* 63e, No. 3 (February 1969): 73–104.

Glanc, Tomáš (ed.). *Roman Jakobson. Formalistická škola a dnešní literárni věda ruská.* Prague: Academia, 2005.

Hadden, Cuthbert J. *Haydn.* Letchworth: J.M. Dent & Company, 1902. Project Gutenberg: https://www.gutenberg.org/files/3788/3788-h/3788-h.htm.

Hebdige, Dick. *Subculture: The Meaning of Style.* London and New York: Routledge, 1979.

Hegel, Georg Wilhelm Friedrich. *Aesthetics: Lectures on Fine Art,* Volume II. Translated by T.M. Knox. Oxford: Clarendon Press, 1975.

Hensher, Philip. "The Life of René Magritte Was Even More Surprising Than His Art." *Spectator* November 26, 2021. https://www.spectator.co.uk/article/the-life-of-ren-magritte-was-even-more-surprising-than-his-art.

Jakobson, Roman. *My Futurist Years,* compiled and edited by Bengt Jangfeldt and Stephen Rudy. Translated by Stephen Rudy. New York: Marsilio Publishers, 1997.

Jakobson, Roman, and Moris Halle. *Fundamentals of Language.* Berlin and New York: Mouton de Gruyter, 1956.

Jakobson, Roman, and Krystyna Promorska. *Dialogues.* Cambridge MA: MIT Press, 1988.

Ottinger, Didier. *Nom d'une pipe! ou Comment Magritte r êva d'expédier Hegel en vacances.* Paris: L'Échoppe, 2007.

Siren, Jana. *On Imbricate Relations: Between Children's Books Visuality and the Structuralist Moment in East-Central Europe from the 1910s to 1960s.* Espoo: Aalto University, Master's Thesis, 2022. https://aaltodoc.aalto.fi/handle/12345 6789/115365.

Smith, Anne-Marie. *Julia Kristeva: Speaking the Unspeakable.* London: Pluto Press, 1988.

Trimbur, John. *The Call to Write.* Boston MA: Cengage Learning, 2013.

Toman, Jindřich. *Příběh jednoho moderního projektu.* Prague: Karolinum, 2011.

Westwood, Vivienne, and Ian Kelly. *Vivienne Westwood*. London: Picador, 2014.

Whittle, Michael. "The Mechanism of Meaning: The Diagrammatic Genius of Arakawa and Gins." *Diagrammatology: Diagrams in Art and Culture* (Blog). 20.4.2017. https://www.michael-whittle.com/diagrammatology/the-mechanism-of-meaning-the-diagrammatic-genius-of-arakawa-and-gins.

Wimsatt, William K. and Beardsley, Monroe C. "The Intentional Fallacy." *The Sewanee Review* 54, No. 3 (Jul–Sep 1946): 468–488.

Zavacká, Marína, "Dobrodružstvá akademickej mobility: Roman Jakobson na Slovensku." *Historický časopis* 66, No. 1 (January 2018): 107–132.

2   Sketching Out the Structure of the Scenes

What are scenes made of? During our introductory ride and the three career stories we shared in Chapter 1, we have already made some remarks about scenes. But what is the relationship between, for example, communities and scenes? This we deal with in this chapter, in "Communities and/vs Scenes – and Scene People," which also studies some major agents of the extended communities or post-communities that scenes are. In "Visible Popular Scenes," we dive into (in)famous scenes of popular culture and the kinds of questions and facts they raise for the study. It would be helpful to get a better taxonomical grip on the topic. And this we aim to do, together with a broad array of (partly miscellaneous) notes on how scenes work, in the major part of the chapter, "Taxonomizing Scenes." This last part of this chapter deals with structures, currents, and peculiarities of scenes, so that we can understand them better.

Communities and/vs Scenes – and Scene People

We have all been members of communities, where we have had a hands-on understanding of the people who we are dealing with. Communities like clubs, associations, neighbors, and just friends, small networks of people, partly make us who we are. They build us, like scenes, but the latter are not just a handful of people who we somehow can control and make sense of in our minds and experience. Even if we talk about communities through bigger units, like neighborhoods, districts, or, for example, "the African American community" of Philadelphia, it is still about networks of people. They might share what is typical of scenes, the way we swim in bigger ponds with a lot of people we do not actually know, but there is something more to scenes, the need to use the word, for example, about the theater scene of Athens or the music scene of Cairo. Scenes are not just more accessible. You can just fly in and hang out for a week in the clubs of Istanbul, and take a look at the "scene," but they are also "scenes," i.e. places to show off, distribute culture, be "on stage" with people, and they exist geographically in one place, in a network of venues. The Zoo is part of Berlin, but any downtown café is more connected

DOI: 10.4324/9781003412786-3

to any Berlin art or popular culture scene. They are the same everywhere, but different. There is the music scene of Warsaw and the music scene of Krakow, and anyone understands what the word scene means there. Still, only those who have hung out in them know the difference. Scenes share a lot, from cafés to institutional venues, but everywhere there are specialties and different accents on how scenes work.

Sometimes scenes are unique. We know only of one strong glass art scene, and it is (still) in Murano, Venice. And although Argentina more broadly, and many places in the world, host some kind of a tango scene, people in the "business" think that Buenos Aires is The scene, and they all, if they are serious enough, travel there.

To be an insider in a scene, one has to be a member of a community or network of people, strongly, but not all people are insiders in scenes. On the spot, there are always people who just follow the scene and might not know anyone or just a handful of people, but who still have access to the scene. If you flew to Quito today, you could probably find in an hour a couple of internet pages on how to get to grips with the music scene, where to go, and how to land in the most interesting neighborhoods and venues. Communities are harder to get into, even if we're talking about big communities. While small communities might crave engagement and ties, even bigger ones crave settling and/or time spent. Scenes, on the other hand, as extended communities of culture, have space reserved just for the audience. In a way, anyone can walk in.

While scenes do not crave engagement and ties in the same way, to be an insider in them, you have to know people. You can enter the famous diverse music scene of Nairobi by just traveling there and buying tickets, hanging out for a couple of nights, and having a couple of chats. But this will not make you a member of any community in the scene. You have seen the scene, though.

In a scene, some people hang out without any sense of belonging. They can even be hostile toward the scene – many artists in Vienna hate the Vienna scene, we have noticed – but they work in the scene, and might even have an important role on the stage of its life. In the same way, they can be around for years without any active or visible role, but they still somehow belong to the scene.

Everyone in the scene is a part of its audience, public, but some people are only audience, and some people are also active makers, and so have a role in what Howard Becker calls "art worlds." Every scene has many communities and many networks, communities that extend into each other. Otherwise, we would not call it a scene, but maybe a community. For example, in London, the art scene is constantly formed by the communities bred and backed up by art schools and universities, the immigrant communities, and the people that run cultural institutions. In all these tribes, people feel more belonging than in the overall scene, which they might even become conscious of only when they relocate. More than once, we have heard someone saying that when they moved they realized how bad or good the atmosphere of the old scene was: "But then I understood that I could do anything I want!"

Your main community might consist of the more conservative and bourgeois art people, but at openings you see other fractions of the scenes – and you might have clashes with their opinions in panel discussions, magazines, and events. You recognize them as being in the same scene, although you would not buy just anything they say. Scenes are about a loose structure, more flee-floating, most of their "members" often being only loosely connected to each other and not feeling much belonging. They also produce – and this motivated the writing of this book – sensitivities and sensibilities, without forgetting boundaries and tastes.

One could think of the scene as a platform of its communities and the people who show interest toward it – a bit like we have been taught to discuss art in a certain country, for example (scenes are more accurate and real units of culture). Even more, significant scenes have their own understanding of aesthetics and some sort of system of artistic values. While nationalist institutionalism has nearly everywhere made us think of, for example, Hungarian painting or British contemporary art, nations are not really effective as frames for understanding what happens in culture, although "national states" work hard to bring together cultural worlds with grants, national institutions, and media. Scenes are a natural way to understand, for instance, popular music or painting, as they really, really happen in a scene, develop in a scene, and become first appreciated (if ever) in a scene. It is fantastic how people can suddenly debate Mozart's librettos in a bar, late at night, in Vienna – and it is remarkable how artists from Hong Kong and Beijing know their calligraphy so well. It is fantastic how many pop stars the Stockholm music scene has produced. And, likewise, if we could choose one historical scene to travel to, we might choose the noise, ritual, and butoh-driven Tokyo scene of the 1960s, which must have been dynamic.

The people who are known in scenes are an interesting issue. Some are known by everyone, practically speaking, but then there are many who have key roles, but are somehow invisible. Some producers and curators are like that. Only real insiders know how much they have impact on a scene.

Some audience members are just audience members, like most buyers of design in Milan. They might be visitors and tourists, who know the scene because of a tourist guide or through a friend's recommendation. They possess basic knowledge on what places they must visit. In Vienna the same kind of tourists, if they prefer visual art, go to Kunsthistorisches Museum, Belvedere, and Albertina or the Museums Quartier. Classical music lovers never forget to visit Mozarthaus, at least one expensive concert in Musikverein and opera or ballet in Staatsoper. Fans of turbofolk and Balkan culture spend a lot of time at Ottakringer Strasse. After a couple of days at the place, tourists and visitors usually do not understand very well what is really going on at the scene. Still, they should be considered as an important and integral part of it. Scenes that lack the big artistic venues, imperial buildings, and various popular attractions have very different atmospheres, of course, than metropolises dealing with millions of tourists every year. Then there are the locals. They can be divided into two groups – one with interest and knowledge about the scene (these people might be even insiders), and another without any deeper understanding about what is happening there. All these people buy design in Milan. They visit the main venues and enjoy the well-working distribution system of the city's design scene.[1] Some are professionals, for example, critics, or people who have some connection to the scene. Some want to keep a distance; some desire to be insiders, if they are not yet. The latter are sometimes like hangers-on at motorcycle clubs. They want to represent some part of the scene. Where bands rehearse, openings flourish, and writers discuss over a cup of coffee, many outsiders or semi-outsiders of scenes hang out to get a taste of its DNA.

Members of professional scene communities are those who are, for example, teaching in an MA music program in the city or playing in the house band of a central club. They might be passive socially, and not go to other gigs or venues, but they have a role. Some might even hate being in the scene, and they might fight its paradigms, but their destiny, maybe through their place of living and their network, is to be part of the Berlin art scene or the St. Petersburg theater scene. We recognize leaders of scene communities, key art writers and critics, and directors of cultural institutions. But then there are also scene persons, i.e. they are key persons of a scene without any visible reason, but still are somehow, strongly, notable figures. Their main role in art is that they are somehow present in scenes, for example, actively at every opening, or being a muse for different artists. We say that they "know everyone" (which is not, of course, literally true) or that this is a "guy you should know." Key people can have made it internationally. Some are somewhat mythical, with a celebrity aura in their own scene. All these roles sum up the way scenes work agent-wise. The powerful ones, the loud critics, the big buyers, the influencers, and the gray workers can, of course, be the same person, but no scene works without a variety of core persons who are professionals and/or part of the publics at the heart of its activity.

Visible Popular Scenes

Changes in the appearance, power-relations, and importance of scenes show something significant about their role in popular culture. The way West Coast rap became a thing, after the long dominance of New York's original, historically foundational rap scene, in the 1990s was really a visible emergence of a new scene, as the concept of "gangsta rap" entered popular culture. Although it was called "West Coast," everyone in the field understood that it was about the metropolitan area of Los Angeles, and often even just about a smaller area, ranging from Long Beach to Compton on the southside of the city proper. Originally, we were talking about a relatively small urban area. For rap fans it really became clear that two scenes were fighting each other during the mid-1990s, as not just the Source Awards in 1995, held in New York, became a provocative battle of speeches, but as also Biggie Smalls and Tupac Shakur were shot in the aftermath of the verbal clashes. Even Wikipedia has its own page for "East Coast – West Coast hip hop rivalry," focusing on the competition of two "scenes" and visually the quarrel became iconic through (the West Coast duo) The Dogg Pound's *New York New York* video, where the rappers were like Godzillas walking and jumping around between New York's skyscrapers – and Snoop Doggy Dog, visiting the video, even destroyed some. Rap fans were privileged scene-wise, as they could see clearly, through the clash, how much the development of their music in the US was about the competition and difference of two scenes which were also aesthetically relatively different. If New York's more openly politicized rap music had a noisy background and a fast, circulating rhythm, the West Coast presented juicier sounds, a slower beat, and politically speaking one could think they stepped closer to literary realism (Victor Hugo style) with their raw depictions of street life. Of course, the (in)famous East and West Coast scenes did not represent all scenes in their respective areas, but just the communities associated with certain visible elements of culture, that defined the difference. Still, for a fan of rap music, this made the impact and nature of scenes obvious.

As if this was not enough, Southern hip-hop also appeared as its own genre in the 1990s, as a set of scenes like Atlanta, Houston, and later Miami, and it was portrayed as a cluster of scenes by both the music industry and critics. But the most important thing to raise scene consciousness was anyway the East vs. West clash, and still today, many who are into hip hop listen to certain "scenes" and talk about their interest in that fashion. Rap, as a very urban phenomenon, so gained even more of a scene-driven nature, very openly, a thing which would never have been the case if there had not been a quarrel to discuss, a quarrel that led to artists performing the difference in a variety of ways in their work. The same kind of moments of truth, that, of course, have also been moments when scenes have mattered more than they usually matter, including, for example, the relocation of the continental contemporary art scene to New York after the Second World War or the way some parts of the Anglophone rock music scene became a thing in West Berlin in the 1980s (Nick Cave, David Bowie). At the same time, it is often hard to understand in smaller cities, how even townships can function as platforms for scenes. Some cities are just too big and too active. The New York rap scene was originally just a scene in a small area in The Bronx, and when Blondie made rap more known to the masses with "Rapture" (1980), it was a big issue for the expansion of the music and the culture, although on the underground the distance from Central Manhattan to the key corners of The Bronx was just a half-hour ride.

Cities and sometimes even small fractions of cityscapes support very different "soundtracks of our lives," which become your everyday life thing, whether you're in the music scene or not. Kwaito, South African house music, might dominate the air in Johannesburg. Jùjú and yo-pop might dwell in your ears for weeks after leaving Lagos.

It is not just that scenes make possible certain moves, or provide paradigms, their own classics, or energies, atmospheres, and whatever, but they also give shade and shelter in different ways. People from the Teheran art scene testify the importance of the communities united under the umbrella of contemporary art, and their political support for equality and free thinking.

In many places, even the law supports the autonomy of the art scenes, through the Western conception of art as a territory for relative freedom and autonomy. Countries have laws, but cities have rules and policies, too. In many places, one can work even against copyright if one's work is legitimate in the scene. One of us was once invited to court to testify that a work challenging and testing the boundaries of copyright issues was "art."

The etymology of the term scene is illuminative. The Greek *skene* was a building behind the stage, a hut for changing masks and costumes, during the performance a background for the acts (Latin *scena*). The original word had its root in *skia*, shadow, i.e. something that gives shade (σκιά). Scenes do give shade. They provide shelter, not just for a community, as scenes often consist of a variety of even mutually conflicting communities, but for a whole cultural realm.

In this book, we work with this concept mainly in the meaning of the particular sphere or area of activity and the people who are somehow involved in it. Among these spheres, we will be particularly interested in an area in this context that is in any way related to art and artistic activities. Although we are aware of the social significance of the skateboarder scenes in major Western cities, gastronomic (Paris, New York) or club scenes (London, Baltimore) in certain cities, and on the other hand, the potentials that a strong hippie or hipster scene or a violent political activist scene can bring out, the framework of art will be exceeded only exceptionally, and mainly through our discourse on intellectual scenes, which we started already with our notes on Roman Jakobson's work, as art scenes are so strong and for us easy to cover.

We already worked out a differentiation of what is mainly meant by the concept of communities. The art scene also needs to be distinguished from subcultures, because they are certainly not synonyms, although in some cases they may relate to quite the same group of people. An art scene or a popular culture scene cannot at least as a whole be reduced to just a subculture. The art scene includes not only creators and artists, or fans or spectators but also the entire "cultural" infrastructure and art institutions. It is also true that what subcultures produce does not always have an artistic form, as Dick Hebdige points out:

> Subcultures are not "cultural" in this sense, and the styles with which they
> are identified cannot be adequately or usefully described as "art of a high

degree". Rather they manifest culture in the broader sense, as systems of communication, forms of expression and representation. [...] subcultural styles do indeed qualify as art but as art in (and out of) particular contexts; not as timeless objects, judged by the immutable criteria of traditional aesthetics, but as "appropriations", "thefts", subversive transformations, as movement.[2]

It should also be emphasized that subcultures can be very different in different scenes. Punks in London were often coming from a working-class background, while politically they belonged to the radical left. Their influence on the cultural scene of London was enormous, especially in the seventies and eighties. In contrary, punks in post-communist Bratislava of the 1990s belonged mainly to the middle class. Their views could often be described as right-wing, sometimes even racist. Compared to London, their cultural influence was weak and almost invisible.

If we talk about the scene in the case of Jakobson, it is largely an intellectual scene, whether in Moscow, Prague, or New York. Undoubtedly, he also felt it natural to work in the art scene, at least as far as the environment of the Moscow avant-garde was concerned, although he was not unknown to art circles in Prague, either. As for Vivienne Westwood, the direct connection to the art scene and the fashion scene is much stronger, as her work responded to what happened in music, visual culture, and design. Magritte is all about art scenes in the narrow meaning of the concept. Although these are markedly different examples, they have in common the fact that they have intervened in the scenes in such a fundamental way that it marked not only the local community, but a significant part of the art global world. This, though, would not have happened without strong scenes that backed up it all.

Taxonomizing Scenes

When one is in a visual arts scene, there are artists, curators, gallerists, mediators, museum professionals, collectors, and elevated hangouts around – without forgetting critics. Sometimes the same individual can have many of these roles at the same time. Still, the interesting thing is that if one is an artist, one might not have anything to do with critics, have never met them, and might know them only from texts they write. And even major artists don't necessarily know the people from the main museums. Some art museum professionals do not have any contact with the grassroots scene. Still, one accepts the idea that these people are a part of the same scene, and one often knows them – although the thing with scenes referred to as communities is that one is not able to know all the people. The cluster of scenes inside of the big scene – visual arts, film, and literature subscenes – sometimes become in themselves clusters of small scenes, like, for example, political film-makers vs. non-political film-makers. In some cities, we talk about language and culture as decisive for the splitting of scenes. In Riga, there used to be one rap scene in Latvian, another in Russian. Literature scenes in (often huge) Indian cities share English, but the works might be written and/or performed in Hindi, Tamil, and/or Urdu.

We already touched upon different subscenes of art scenes (dance, film) and some major distinctions that conceptually help us claim knowledge about scenes. One new take on this concerns the way scenes are differently interpreted, especially in music. For some a scene means, for instance, the way cultural products are organized, mainly music, and the community that supports this – for example, the country music scene or the noise music scene,[3] and to some extent, of course, "local scenes" are also part of this discussion, which is very much connected to 1950s and 1960s discussions on subculture.[4] For us it still, as a meaningful thing that brings cultural sensitivities and sensibilities together, must be geographical. The broader scenes we do not intuitively even read to be foundational and constitutive in the same way as we read, in everyday speech, geographical scenes to have this role and impact. Maybe post-internet artists find it natural to have their scene just on the internet, but this is an anomaly. One can think that people who use computers a lot in a way live in a corner of the internet, but this does not apply to most people.

One often refers to scenes when explaining the career of an artist. When the Louisiana Museum of Modern Art in Copenhagen published a catalog text on the (originally) Japanese visual artist Yayoi Kusama and her arrival in the West, they wrote that "[s]he came into New York's 1960s art scene as almost a female counterpart to Andy Warhol, expressing herself in a mixture of art, fashion, and happenings."[5] The scene here provides a point for interpretation. And interestingly, the Tokyo scene is virtually never discussed in the West in the case of Kusama, although the work of the Ota Fine Arts gallery had a key role in supporting her rise to international success. Anyway, if Kusama had arrived in Prague and not New York from Tokyo, the museum curators would probably have compared her work to Czechoslovakian graphics. One does not think that arriving with a country hit on a 'national' country scene works in the same way. One might be the new Johnny Cash, but it is more about media and a looser structure, more about just commercially glued platforms, than the glocal post-community with its often alternative or shady spaces that we desire to describe and analyze here. In scenes as geographical entities, many places are not for making or distributing culture, but for just being and/or talking, like cafés.

There are language questions concerning scenes. Some are monolingual, some bilingual – and some host many languages, maybe brought together by one dominant, possibly foreign (colonial) language, like English in historical British colonies. When the poet Henry Parland settled in Helsinki in the early twentieth century, he realized that there was a more flourishing Swedish-language poetry scene – so he decided to learn Swedish before

Finnish.[6] In Kampala, the capital of Uganda, a country with 43 existing living languages, people find their way to poetry as much as rap music, and that it can't be too much of an issue that a person is sometimes lost as they don't get the spoken or written language.

There are also major and minor art scenes, and sometimes history forgets the minor ones and their impact, as the larger ones manifest their importance more easily on the pages of history. Tom Sandqvist's *Dada East* (2006) writes in the story of Tristan Tzara, the founder of Dadaism, who left Romania (he was born in *Moineşti)* for Zurich in 1915, that Dada clearly had Romanian roots. Sandqvist's main claim, which he defends well, is that Dada would have been a thing already in Eastern Europe, a mix of the Romanian cultural spirit and Yiddish tradition, and that it would have migrated to Zurich quite well-formed already.[7]

Some scenes do not have a long history. Scenes might also be present for only a short period of the year, the same people popping up again, maybe after 11 and a half months. Curator Paco Barragan once said about Miami, "There is no art scene in Miami. The art fair is like a UFO that lands every year for a week." The fair is too big and too loose to be a community. It is not, of course, a scene in the basic sense, but it has a place and quite a permanent community, so it maybe inhabits some of the typical traits of scenes. Scenes have different levels of permanence and inertia.

Scenes also compete and are compared. Plenge Jakobsen writes, "There is no doubt that over the past ten years Oslo has had the most vital and interesting art scene in Scandinavia" (*Kunstkritikk*, 10.5.2013). No doubt, artists and curators in Stockholm or Copenhagen would not necessarily buy this (and we doubt that Jakobsen studied well all Scandinavian art scenes before making the claim), but it says a lot about the way we view scenes. Some are better. Often, their histories and reputations produce expectations. We have heard countless times someone explaining things like "then X happened; it was really a Y experience," Y here standing for a certain scene: "It is a must to visit the 798 art zone when in Beijing. Otherwise, you have not even seen the city!"

What is central for different scenes is sometimes, though, not based only on who's there permanently. For example, the Madrid art scene is what it is partly because of the old colonial relations and traffic connections – airplanes – that take the Latin American art scene there, more than to any other city in Europe. This commuting is a thing in the scene. Visiting the ARCO, the Madrid Art Fair, is for most European art dealers, critics, and curators the biggest glimpse of South American art that they'll ever get – but this art has a permanent presence in the city, although the artists do not necessarily live there (although this happens, of course, too, supported by the shared language). In the same way, areas that were once connected as Yugoslavia are not just close to each other, but they all shared the same country and its capital, Belgrade, long ago as their main scene. Still, people from Ljubljana (Slovenia) know what is going in

Belgrade (Serbia) not just following the closeness of the countries and cities, but the age-old connections (that, of course, existed even before Yugoslavia) and structural pathways that once connected everything into one whole, that used to have an intense life in Belgrade, the capital of Yugoslavia. Art schools and their exchange programs, the networks of key characters of the scene, and cheap airline connections – and other traffic connections – spice up the permanent structures.[8]

We also again want to accentuate that scenes rise and fall. Now New York is getting too costly to live in, so young artists move to Austin, Detroit, Miami, Seattle, and other major cities in the US. Vienna was once a fantastic world city with its flourishing, diverse artistic scene – and Bucharest was called Little Paris – but there is an end to all flourishing, and cities and scenes change, too. They have different extensions, as well. St. Petersburg is huge as an art scene, but it is closed and it does not reach out – and Helsinki is small but reaches out a lot, partly because of state funding that makes it easy to go abroad and the open, upbeat Western cultural system, with people speaking English well.

It is not too much said if one puts it this way: scenes die, too. "There used to be a great art scene in pre-war Bucharest," someone said to us. Flourishing scenes make people move in and build lives and careers, and when the scenes are flourishing, only a major change will make people quit coming. Although all scenes need "locals," too, they are never only products of the locals. People travel in for "business" – but more importantly, as already discussed in the Introduction and Chapter 1, they migrate in. When things start going in the wrong direction, people also start moving out fast. If young artists have in the US moved to cities that did not ring a bell in the artworld some years ago, Russian scenes, especially close to the Western border (St. Petersburg) are spreading out globally right now as artists flee the country, and some parts of it are going underground following the political pressure. People seek to find their relatives and networks, and subscenes with Ukrainians and Russians get many new "members."

We know why our politically active artist friends move to Berlin (there is a political art scene). And we know that refugees have always been important for big art scenes. Big cities, big scenes – they are places where at least, in principle, anyone can land easily. This, of course, increases their allure in art communities. We are quite convinced we can somehow land well in Istanbul, Tokyo, Rio, or Lagos – but we doubt our chances in the tiny towns of Salem (US) or Cēsis (Latvia).

Every scene has its waves – feminist, postcolonial, and whatever – and they happen at different times following different needs, as scenes have different audiences with different local urges, and they have different connections, low-cost airlines and old social connections (like the ones that remain in Yugoslavia and in the IVY countries although the old states are gone). Some scenes are political, for a while or permanently – and some host a sense of beauty and interest in serving the people, too, not just the élite and the scene members. It is incredible how different scenes can be in this sense, although on the surface they can look quite the same. Noise music and pop painting tsunamis have blown through Tokyo many times. Kabul once had an art scene, but unfortunate wars and civil wars have left the remains of what once existed shattered all over the place, when not in exile. Exhibitions happen in foreign cultural institutes. Some say that street art flourishes. Copenhagen in the early 2000s was a city where one could make an artistic career just by debating on different semi-political panels in the lecture halls of art museums – while the political and economic situation of the country was as stable as it could be. Landing in these scenes can be very different, although one would find the same kind of circles hidden in all the aforementioned cities, just with different importance.

Sometimes the theater scene is undeveloped or dead, sometimes visual arts. Sometimes there is clearly a leading scene inside of the scene; i.e. the music scene can be strong and it leads the whole art scene, or an intellectual scene can be driven by a philosophy scene. There can be a strong visual art scene together with a strong music scene – but accompanied by a craft scene and a cirque nouveau scene. And the art scene can be connected to some sport, like (dance and) figure skating. The possibilities are endless.

Scenes teach us. It is not just that we get habituated to certain sorts of sensibilities, atmospheres, conventions, leading figures, and their art – but that what we learn about art can really come only from one scene, plus the addition of the DVDs, TV programs, occasional festival visits, etc., that accompany it. And many people in the scene teach, not just in the art schools of the scene. There are seminars, panel discussions, and reading groups. There are student theaters and preparatory art schools that can have a huge impact on the scene – and even galleries that are pedagogically driven, or just active individuals, who see their work as being to spread the joy of theater or design to everyone.

Philosophers learned in mid-twentieth-century Parisian cafés more than they learned in universities – and in many of these dialogical platforms of scenes of art and intellectual culture one continues the culture of the *salons* that Jürgen Habermas coined for the start for public sphere, and that initially also had a role in the invention of art as a concept and institution.[9]

Pedagogically schools can, of course, sometimes, if they are strong enough, become the hearts and guts of a whole scene – practically being the whole scene, only collecting the remains of other cultural practices around them. Did the small town of Vitebsk in today's Belarus have an art scene in the early twentieth century? When one reads about suprematist and other early modernist art at the time, the school there looks strong, as Marc Chagall and Kazimir Malevich taught there. But it is really hard to say today what happened in the town later on, as we don't really document scenes. Also, the Black Mountain College might look later on like a scene, although, organized around John Dewey's ideas on education, Jozef Albers, Walter Gropius, Cy Twombly, Robert Raushcenberg, Merce Cunningham, John Cage, and Willem de Kooning did not really live in North Carolina, but came there from their own scene (New York) for shorter periods.

Occasionally, someone who could really be considered to be a product of their scene, becomes "big" somewhere else – but remains overlooked in the original scene. When one of us was interviewing an Italian philosopher in the early 2000s, a name that had already broken the glass ceiling in the US and most of Western Europe, Giorgio Agamben, was mentioned. The interviewed scholar nodded, and said: "Oh, the Italian guy that you read in other countries. I have heard about him." This was a comment that was probably placed without any intention to mock or degrade Agamben, although it was made by someone who had stature locally. It was probably more of a curious comment, like questioning why this figure had been picked up from the (notably rich) Italian philosophical scene (rotating around Milan, from where many key personalities of intellectual culture take trains to the universities of Bologna and Verona). It might have included a sour side taste of the, "you could have chosen better" type. Something of the same type of thing happened with Jacques Derrida. Being in some sense the utmost example of French philosophy's playfulness, lack of answers and clear argumentation, and cryptic way of writing, it is somewhat absurd how, although known by everyone in the Parisian scene, he became "someone" first in the US, in literary criticism, and then, also in other European countries. He wasn't living in the center of the Paris as other big names – Foucault, Roland Barthes, and Claude Levi-Strauss. Iranian film people sometimes say that Abbas Kiarostami is not very interesting, and that his work is something that "Westerners like."[10] Outsiders who are big "somewhere else" ("big in Japan" used to be a term in hard rock music) are one key figure in the global system of cultural scenes.

The way works of art gain different readings and how they provoke different kinds of reactions in different scenes is interesting. Stories about how the Milanese audience accepts or does not accept certain singers or composers in the opera by whistling and/or booing, how the American theater audience in New York met performances they disliked by throwing fruit in the nineteenth century, and how the Helsinki theater audience sits quite still without showing reactions during a performance (still being more 'alive' than in other Finnish cities) are about different cultural, sometimes scene-driven ways of reacting to things – as much as the way African American audiences (as subscenes of large cities in the US) have famously produced the call-and-response reaction, i.e. the way the singer asks them things and they shout back, something that rock culture adopted later on.

Still, even more, the destiny of works of art is, besides the cultural context and the work of the professionals (producers, theater or musical directors, performers) who bring it to a new place, and besides trivialities like one active member of the audience can laugh a lot and make others laugh, too, or that a performance can luckily or not that luckily be shown at a festival after a very positively or negatively provoking performance, also something that leads back to the scenes. Sometimes it is hard to say why a work finds itself in different positions in different scenes.

Anssi Pulkkinen's *Street View (Reassembled)* (2017) was a sculptural work, in a sense a sculptural intervention, that broke the circle of bourgeois and nationalist monument culture in Finland by winning a competition. In his work for the Mobile Home competition, Pulkkinen took a destroyed house from Syria, recreated standing on a truck, which like refugees during those years traveled around Europe on the back of it. The work was met by locals in Aleppo with applause: "show them what happens here!" The work was first met with emphatic seriousness in Copenhagen and Amsterdam, then with profound interest in Sweden – but when it hit Finland, several attacks were launched against the artist, who was claimed to "use" the war and its material for his own "artistic tripping."[11] In discussions with the artist and commissioners no answer was found for this. There was a discussion at a fair where the work was shown, and everyone was perplexed. We tried to analyze the way the sculpture was shown – in some cities entering a marketplace, for example, on the car and in Helsinki being shown at an interior design fair – there is a difference here – but in the end it was impossible to come up with a solution. One can speculate whether it was just that the scenes were different, ready, and/or not ready for different types of artworks, or overtly sensitive to certain attitudes. Maybe the Stockholm scene had already undergone a fierce discussion about the role of privileged artists and/or their way of also asking the people involved what they think (they were positive in Pulkkinen's case) – or then Helsinki had seen too many of this type of work, which made it hard to penetrate it with one more of this type. Maybe Pulkkinen was too much of a local artist in Helsinki (sometimes it helps to come from another scene)? No one is a prophet in their own land, as they say. Or, the Amsterdam scene might have been more activist in the context where the work was presented, and coming to Helsinki kind of nailed it to a certain corner of the art scene, in the design scene, which was the wrong place for it.

Whatever, scenes have different atmospheres, and take in or push out certain materials, like chemical substances. In Helsinki in the late 2010s, the appropriation discussion was totally overheated – mainly following the Indigenous art community's (the Sami) attacks on the way their culture, especially their clothes, was often (ab)used by the mainstream art scene in Helsinki (over 600 miles from the areas roamed by them). The work of Pulkkinen might have hit this very complicated and sensitive button of who can make use of other people's suffering, although what Pulkkinen did was to turn a whole phenomenon, statues, and monuments, into political art, and although he had support from the people who were involved with the Syrian war. Another aspect might have been that in other cities there might have been Syrian activists and artists involved in some of situations where the work was presented, or other notable political figures of the scene – which was lacking in the Helsinki presentation of the work.

There are incredible historical examples of a work meeting totally different responses. When the first British Shakespeare company arrived in New York in 1849 with the at the time still quite new "highbrow" interpretation of the playwright, the audience, that had gotten used to a more popular Shakespeare (probably the more traditional one), which was freely used to convey local and contemporary issues, and which was not exegetical nor sublimely recited by its nature, booed the play totally, and, to get back to reactions by the audiences, and the cultural differences that are at stake in this, threw not just rotten tomatoes and fruit, but also chairs at the actors.[12] This led to a counterattack by the bourgeois and elitist New York art scene, who so much desired to have a British highbrow Shakespeare among themselves, that they, together with the police, organized a new take on this that ended up in the infamous Astor Place riot. Over 50 people died in the brawl, and the theater house was partly destroyed. Then highbrow Shakespeare started its victorious trail in the US, which was to become overshadowed only by Hollywood films, when they took up the English classic. Like already mentioned, René Magritte's work became something only when he relocated his career to Paris – and in the end this happened to all his works that he had produced in Belgium.

Who knows, later on, what the presence or an artist does in these kind of situations, what the role of the presenter, producer, or curator could be (some curators have more freedom than others to do what they want), but the differences must sometimes lead to histories of scenes, their power relations, their energies, frustrations, and readiness for new things, especially the kinds that a new artist or a work of art entails. Moving to new places, artworks can gain a pinch of exotic atmosphere. The Finnish author Arto Paasilinna, who was in Finland mainly a somewhat respected popular writer who touched upon stereotypical themes that the highbrow scene did not that much appreciate, became in France, through the acceptance of the Paris scene, a mystical person, a man of the woods, like an indigenous celebrity, and his books sold a lot. But, for sure, who can say which scene is right about an author, whether we are talking about Paasilinna or Agamben? Even if the work of Paasilinna, for example, felt a bit too simple and stereotypical for a Finn who was marinated in the highbrow literary scene of Helsinki, would they have the right to say more about it than a Parisian connoisseur? In the original scenes, people often think that they have the right to judge the artist more than in others.

And like we think (maybe even too much) about people representing their nations or broader linguistico-culturally defined cultures, we also think of them as representing scenes more than could ever be said just about networks. Nirvana might be seen as an American rock band, but Seattle and its grunge scene is what really profiles it – and the same could be said about Paris and Picasso: although Picasso was Spanish, it is Paris that defines him as an artist, his learnings there and the possibilities offered by the Parisian art scene.

The same interpretation of scenes as cultures marks Diana Ross's belonging to the Detroit music scene and the Motown pop that was at the heart of the enterprise there – the whole world with performance joints, and even more record companies, and famous studio musicians. And although we might think of David Bowie as truly British, his adventures in the dark West Berlin scene of the late 1970s, that made his music more synth-based, are what made him partly what we know today, and this is how people who are into this type of music read him and his story as an artist.

What is interesting is that one cannot really do the same things in different scenes. They provide us with very different boundaries, besides the different potentials they are full of. You cannot do much openly politically if you are working in Moscow or Minsk today, and there are countless cities where open commercialism is a definite no – at the same time a bit of selling attitude will not be a problem in most of the scenes of London or Cologne. This is about aesthetics, too. Scenes have different readymade audiences that an artist can reach, with differing abilities to interpret and enjoy art – and in scenes different formal artistic practices and traditions dominate. To gain taste, we need training and some sort of habituation. If you have never been into reggae music, living in Brixton (for a couple of months) might change it. If you hear it every day at the underground station and through the wall from the neighbor's house, you start gaining the structures, the way of expression, and the differences inside of the musical genre. This is how scenes work. The eye becomes sensitive to graphic pop painting in Bratislava, minimalist design in Helsinki, and mainstream fashion in chic but never too fashion-radical Stockholm. This is the reason why many artists desire and decide to move to another scene, and the relocations are typical for artist biographies and even artist statements.[13] If I was interested in making it in salsa, Havana or Miami could soon be my home.

It is as fascinating that some cities and their scenes are famous – but some are equally infamous or thought to be nothing scene-wise. Some scenes could be said to be referential. Think of Paris or New York in visual art – or club music in Manchester or Baltimore. And there are, of course, big contemporary art scenes (Berlin), middle-sized ones (Oslo), and then small scenes (Linz). Referentiality is not about size, though, at least not totally. It might not be important if a film maker is from Oslo or Gothenburg – but Copenhagen is referential, because of the strength and even dogmatic history of the recent Danish film scene.

From time to time, we hear that there is no scene in a certain city or town. In Finland, some people from Turku have been constantly saying that Turku, a town with approximately 200,000 inhabitants and an art school, does not have an art scene. For an outsider, the whole idea sounds crazy, and it looks different – but the experience is there for some, the feeling, that although there is a community, there is no more to it. Even more, Philadelphia is a city, that still for a little over a decade was said to have no real art scene[14] – although there is the University of Arts there with famous teachers and the city hosts 6 million inhabitants in its metropolitan area. In Europe, this would be joke anywhere, but, of course, as New York City is just two hours away, it has been logical that artists have moved out of Philadelphia, at least closer to the NY gallery scene. (Philadelphia might also have been evaluated with unfair criteria, as NY is so close.) Today this has changed, we are told – artists are returning, following the economic problems that have developed following the high cost of living in today's NY. Some say Philadelphia has again an art scene, but this on/off that seems to be the destiny of the city is perplexing for us who are outsiders. It is just too big to be that, in a sense, but the logic follows from being close to one of the world capitals of art. The experience here is an interesting one. What really is the experience of this "lacking a scene"? Some people keep saying this about Indian contemporary art, in Mumbai and Delhi: "The scene is small, if it even exists." Is this about the pressure to exhibit elsewhere – or of people moving constantly away (or, then, returning)? Maybe at least sometimes.

It must have felt weird when the first scene was developing. Partly, one can ask – this is actually what we believe – if Baudelaire's notions on modernity were sometimes notes on the first developing art and intellectual scene, a scene, where suddenly the medieval city and the pre-democratic city space had vanished, where people shared boulevards, there were alternative exhibition spaces (*Salon des refusés*), cafés, and other venues, even its own growing bohemian township (Montmartre), and a growing new way for modern art education and urban life to bring artists and entertainers together (often portrayed in Impressionist painting). In *The Painter of Modern Life*, Baudelaire discusses Parisian culture of the 1860s, changes in modernity that Benjamin then continues to explore in his unfinished *Passagenwerk*, where we have often been looking for overall development, but where one can also find, if interested, notions on a certain scene developing, a space shared by artists, intellectuals, and other scene people, where they see each other in the more open modern city and exchange ideas and impressions.[15]

In the same way, one can find echoes and notes on scenes in Angela McRobbie's views on the development of the cultural market[16] and Mary Jane Jacob's and Michelle Grabner's *The Studio Reader* (2010), with all its collected stories on how people meet in studios, how they present work (this started in the bottega of Renaissance Italy, where craftsmen lived and exhibited), and how they are places to be, not homes, but not totally public, either.[17]

How have some scenes, then, in the end, also become atmospherically interesting? This is an issue that we have no answer for. What are atmospheres? Tonino Griffero calls them "half-things,"[18] and we recognize some of them when reminded or told (sometimes we know them even if we have not visited them). The laid-back, spacy, and grassroots atmosphere of the Berlin art scene is partly due to the nature of the spacy and laid-back nature of the German capital, but it is also about the art that one finds there, often political, often accentuating everyday experimentalism (from hipster to avant-garde), and certain institutions there, from art schools (UDK) to big exhibition spaces. Everyone who has visited the city's scene for a while remembers it, and can feel it – a light breeze of vegetarian food, laid-back joints, and discussions, and a lot of people who have moved in.

Just as the idea of what art is and with it the artworld is constantly changing, so are the art scenes. In the nineteenth century, the community of artists in Paris was made up of completely different artists than in Vienna in the early twentieth century, both of which are nowhere near the London scene of the 1960s, New York at the end of the millennium, or present-day Berlin. Even with a superficial knowledge of each of them, it must be clear to us that these are completely different worlds which, apart being understood as art scenes, have not had much in common artistically speaking.

The differences between them are not only due to the fact that we are comparing art scenes from different historical periods. The local tradition of artistic production, the expectations of the audience, the character, and strength of the institutions, or the favorable political situation play a strong role. Of course, the impact of economic conditions on the development of art cannot be overlooked either.[19] Suffice it to recall how the promotion of the arts significantly changed the art scene in New York in the 1950s, or the impact of investment in culture at the turn of the millennium in London.

Smaller art and cultural scenes often have a relational identity, as they follow the big ones. They are sometimes strong in one genre or field of art, but this is not a necessary condition. Sometimes they are average or even below average in all areas of culture. What sets them apart from the biggest art scenes is mainly that they do not look for the final award in the home scene, in their community and among their local critics. The crucial goal for them is the big scene, where they strive to assert themselves and gain recognition.

Thus, large scenes are foci that fundamentally affect the nature of the artworld and attract actors from all other scenes that are identified by their qualities. Small scenes can usually only come to prominence through one or two sub-scenes, but often only for a short time, when they prevail under favorable circumstances. And those periods become 'golden ages,' endlessly cited examples for local inspiration, and in the end the main source of artistic conservatism.

What helps in the development of both small and large art scenes is that there must be favorable political and social conditions. We can even say that the real development of a scene might be possible only in democratic societies, where the conditions for freedom of expression are guaranteed. Although there are underground art scenes in totalitarian regimes that have exceptional results, such a situation is usually not sustainable in the long run and often does not last long.

But what do cultural scenes (and more commonly scenes) have in common? We have here told stories that show the existence of something that is called a scene, we have nailed differences and a role for the phenomenon, but we haven't so far gone into discussing what keeps them together as a concept.

Traditionally, scenes have been studied in sociology and anthropology as a continuation of traditional community research. We have benefited from reading them and their ideas on class, belonging, and subcultural politics (identity, space, participation),[20] but they do not, in the end, help us very much to understand how scenes could have an aesthetic effect.

Anyway, career-wise, scenes should be the focus of attention for research. Nobody has become a global name in the artworld without being accepted first by a single scene with its single logic. A particular work of art does not exist in a vacuum called the global artworld. Every work of art is first part of an art scene. The art scene can be considered a gateway to the artworld at the same time as it is always a part of it. It was definitely possible to make Andy Warhol's "products" in the New York art scene rather in the Moscow art scene of the 1960s, and, of course, by becoming something in a big scene, one quite naturally becomes an overall name. Big in New York means nearly instantly big anywhere. Where did this evolve and when – the way certain scenes started to mean so much for other scenes, that changes in them nearly automatically became changes in others? Anyway, it is not totally wrong to say that what art and popular culture is, today, globally, at least partly stands on the shoulders of a big bunch of influential scenes and would be different without them.

Knowing scenes, or at least something about them, also enriches our encounters with many historical works – or it can be even crucial to know something about the scene where a work is produced, to make sense of it. For example, Vienna actionism might look totally childish for a Nordic scholar or artist who lives in a non-conservative atmosphere with a free sex life and not much bourgeois culture nor taboos, say. The "Orgies-Mysteries Theater" (1970-) which the member of the group performed infamously at Schloss Prinzdorf, Dionysian feasts where blood and gore were central, ritual

> disembowelment of different animals (bulls, sheep), the act of stuffing entrails back into hacked-open carcasses, pouring blood on actors representing Christ and Oedipus, and night time processions around Prinzdorf with goats, pigs, horses, sheep dogs and cattle, not to mention actors bearing flaming torches,[21]

easily looks pathetic, almost teenage anxiety-driven, if one does not know the political and artistic context that had a presence in Vienna at the time (and partly even now). "One member of the group, Günter Brus, drank his own urine, and sang the Austrian National Anthem while masturbating in another performance, and Hans Cibulka posed with a sliced open fish covering his groin."[22] In a city which was a key city in developing Nazism, where Freud wrote – it has a very neurotic culture – and in a city where strict Catholicism has dominated the cultural scene, this kind of action can, of course, at least to some, find meaningful ground.[23] One can also say that, "some of the more aestheticized installations of Hermann Nitsch reflect so much upon Catholic liturgy and the way it is used in Central Eastern Europe that even stylistically it is hard to grab it without local cultural understanding."[24] One needs to study scenes to understand some of the sides of obscure or weird artworks. Scenes sometimes create them to a high extent. Scenes can be co-authors of artworks.

We are fascinated by the way intellectuals met in the cafés of 1860s Paris and 1920s Vienna and how an alternative rock scene developed in the Berlin of the 1970s. Scenes host lifestyles, rhythms of life, alternative economies, and other matters. A scene is a culturally constitutive thing, which has its own aesthetics – we hurry on to claim (Chapter 5). They are powerhouses of progress and epitomes of the new. We attempt to understand scenes philosophically and artistically. To do this we need to tell stories from scenes. We need to analyze their atmospheres and special traditions and conventions of experience. And we need to delve into many different scenes to paint the big picture.

Notes

1 Howard S. Becker discusses at length the way fully developed "art worlds" provide good distribution systems. Becker, *Art Worlds*, 93.
2 Dick Hebdige, *Subculture: The Meaning of Style* (London and New York: Routledge, 1979), 129.
3 See e.g. Andy Bennett, "Consolidating the Music Scenes Perspective," *Poetics* 32 (2004): 223–234, where local scenes and trans-local scenes also gain attention.
4 See Dick Hebdige, *Subculture*. We are thankful to Giacomo Bottà for helping us out with this issue.
5 Lærke Rydal Jørgensen, Marie Laurberg and Michael Juul Holm, eds., *Yayoi Kusama: In infinity* (Copenhagen. Louisiana Museum of Modern Art, 2015).
6 See e.g. Max Ryynänen, "Henry Parland ja elokuvataide," *Filmihullu* 3 (2001): 18–23.
7 Tom Sandqvist, *Dada East: The Romanians of Cabaret Voltaire* (Cambridge MA: MIT Press, 2006).
8 Silvie Jacobi's work on the way art schools have a local role shows various aspects in the dialogue between an art school and the city where it is situated. Silvie Jacobi, *Art Schools and Place: Geographies of Emerging Artists and Art Scenes* (London: Rowman & Littlefield, 2020).
9 Jürgen Habermas, *The Structural Transformation of the Public Sphere* (Cambridge MA: MIT Press, 1991).
10 We are thankful to Elham Rahmati for this note.
11 More on this: http://www.mobilehome2017.com/fi/. See also Aleksi Malmberg and Annukka Vähäsöyrinki, eds., *Home Re-assembled: On Art, Destruction & Belonging* (Rotterdam: Jap Sam Books, 2017).
12 Lawrence Levine, *Highbrow/Lowbrow: The Emergence of Cultural Hierarchy in America* (Cambridge MA: Harvard University Press, 1988). See Chapter 1.

13 See Rainer Metzinger's *Berlin in the Twenties: Art and Culture 1918–1933* (London: Thames & Hudson, 2007), and its discourse on the impact of expressionism, Dada and cafeterias on the city and its art scene, e.g. 86–101, 99, 253–289.
14 There is a thread in *Quora* about the topic "Does Philadelphia have an Art Scene?" See https://www.quora.com/Does-Philadelphia-have-an-art-scene (visited May 31, 2018; the thread started May 2017).
15 Charles Baudelaire, *The Painter of Modern Life* (London: Penguin, 2010).
16 Angela McRobbie, *Be Creative: Making a Living in the New Culture Industries* (Cambridge: Polity, 2016).
17 Mary Jane Jacob and Michelle Grabner, eds, *The Studio Reader* (Chicago IL: University of Chicago Press, 2010).
18 Tonino Griffero, *Atmospheres: Aesthetics of Emotional Spaces* (New York: Routledge, 2016).
19 Hans van Maanen discusses economic problems in "art worlds" in a very witty way. See Hans van Maanen, *How to Study Art Worlds? On the Societal Functioning of Aesthetic Values* (Amsterdam: Amsterdam University Press, 2009).
20 See Maher, *The Sociology of Scenes*.
21 See Kovalcik and Ryynänen, "The Art Scenes."
22 Ibid.
23 See Eva Badura-Triska, Hubert Klocker, *Vienna Actionism: Art and Upheaval in 1960s' Vienna* (Vienna: Mumok, 2012), 15–25.
24 Ibid. See also Marcin Borchardt, "Viennese Actionism – Transgression as an Art of Social Negation," *Er(r)go. Teoria – Literatura – Kultura* 35, no. 2 (2017): 101–121.

Bibliography

Badura-Triska, Eva, and Klocker Hubert. *Vienna Actionism: Art and Upheaval in 1960s' Vienna.* Vienna: Mumok, 2012.
Baudelaire, Charles. *The Painter of Modern Life.* Translated by P.E. Charvet. London: Penguin, 2010.
Becker, Howard S. *Art Worlds.* Berkeley CA, Los Angeles CA, and London: University of California Press, 1984.
Bennett, Andy. "Consolidating the Music Scenes Perspective." *Poetics* 32 (2004): 223–234.
Borchardt, Marcin. "Viennese Actionism – Transgression as an Art of Social Negation." *Er(r)go. Teoria – Literatura – Kultura* 35, No. 2 (2017): 101–121.
Griffero, Tonino. *Atmospheres: Aesthetics of Emotional Spaces.* New York: Routledge, 2016.
Habermas, Jürgen. *The Structural Transformation of the Public Sphere.* Translated by Thomas Burger. Cambridge MA: MIT Press, 1991.
Hebdige, Dick. *Subculture: The Meaning of Style.* London and New York: Routledge, 1979.
Jacob, Mary Jane, and Michelle Grabner, eds, *The Studio Reader.* Chicago IL: University of Chicago Press, 2010.
Jacobi, Silvie. *Art Schools and Place: Geographies of Emerging Artists and Art Scenes.* London: Rowman & Littlefield, 2020.
Kovalcik, Jozef, and Max Ryynänen. "The Art Scenes." *Contemporary Aesthetics* 16 (2018). https://contempaesthetics.org/newvolume/pages/article.php?articleID=847.
Levine, Lawrence. *Highbrow/Lowbrow: The Emergence of Cultural Hierarchy in America.* Cambridge MA: Harvard University Press, 1988.

50   *Sketching Out the Structure of the Scenes*

Maher, Dana Nell. *The Sociology of Scenes, the Sacramento Poetry Scene.* Las Vegas NV: UNLV Theses, 2009.
Malmberg, Aleksi, and Annukka Vähäsöyrinki, eds., *Home Re-assembled: On Art, Destruction & Belonging.* Rotterdam: Jap Sam Books, 2017.
McRobbie, Angela. *Be Creative: Making a Living in the New Culture Industries.* Cambridge: Polity, 2016.
Metzinger, Rainer. *Berlin in the Twenties: Art and Culture 1918–1933.* London: Thames & Hudson, 2007.
Rydal Jørgensen, Lærke, Marie Laurberg, and Michael Juul Holm, eds., *Yayoi Kusama: In Infinity.* Copenhagen: Louisiana Museum of Modern Art, 2015.
Ryynänen, Max. "Henry Parland ja elokuvataide." *Filmihullu* 3 (2001): 18–23.
Sandqvist, Tom. *Dada East: The Romanians of Cabaret Voltaire.* Cambridge: MIT Press, 2006.
van Maanen, Hans. *How to Study Art Worlds? On the Societal Functioning of Aesthetic Values.* Amsterdam: Amsterdam University Press, 2009.

3 The Scene-Driven Art Theories of Danto and Sontag – And the Urban Thinking of the Twentieth-Century Philosophers

Thinking about the use of Hegel in the Magritte case (presented in Chapter 1), one could imagine that if G.W.F. Hegel lived today, he might not write that culture was born in the East and the development continued to the West – or that the development of art took us from visual art to literature. Some decades ago, he would have probably gone for a more national state-driven approach, but today, as a witty thinker, he could have written a story based on scenes.

When we discuss scenes, it won't be easy to get rid of Hegel's philosophy. A typical example of a Hegelian text that has become an icon for all art scenes, but bases its remarks on only (real and fictional) New York artists and audiences is Arthur C. Danto's "The Artworld" (1964). The text focuses on pop art. Interestingly, maybe indicative of the changes of the times, it saw daylight in the same year as the first monographs on the aesthetics of popular culture, i.e. Umberto Eco's *Apocalittici e integrati* (1964), Susan Sontag's "Notes on Camp" (1964; see below), and not coincidentally, Andy Warhol's exhibition *The Shop* (1964), which took place at the Stable Gallery on Fifth Avenue.

The year 1968 might have been a cultural revolution or just a middle-class revolution fantasy,[1] but 1964, when Timothy Leary published a sign of the times, *The Psychedelic Experience* (1964), seemed to mark a change in our sensitivity. If the crisis of high and low had been noted by Theodor Adorno in 1944 (Culture Industry), where he wrote about the constant tiring desire of people to mash up, e. g. classical music and jazz, 1964, if not yet pointing to the global multiverse of artistic practices, made the issue more concrete and in an open-minded way. Umberto Eco analyzed Superman like any artistic product and wrote a philosophical theory of both kitsch and levels of culture (*basso, medio, alto*). Susan Sontag theorized the increasingly mainstreaming trend concept of camp. The development of pop art, which in the 1950s had featured humorously schizophrenic collages in the work of Richard Hamilton and the one-step trashier, also sculptured, work of Robert Rauchenberg, among others, took the change to new heights in many art scenes.

Philosophically a lot had happened too, like the already-mentioned works by Eco and Sontag. Paul Oskar Kristeller's truly revolutionary essay

DOI: 10.4324/9781003412786-4

"The Modern System of Arts" (Kristeller 1951/1952) showed that there was nothing natural about the concept of art, and that it was quite new (stemming from the mid-eighteenth century), without forgetting that it was a product of a quite arbitrary historical development. On the other hand, the development that had started in the Vienna scene, which we now know as the Vienna Circle, and which rethought philosophy's role in miming models of natural science and conceptual rigidity, had reached a point with Ludwig Wittgenstein where it turned against its early conceptual essentialism. With his ideas on 'family resemblance' – e.g. games do not necessarily share something that would lend them an essentialist definition (*Philosophical Investigations*), but are more like family members who resemble each other – and (connected to the aforementioned) his ideas on language games, notes on discursive patterns which made use of concepts meaningful in different contexts, he pushed Morris Weitz to rethink the definition of art. In Weitz's "The Role of Theory in Aesthetics" (1956) he asked if theory had gone totally wrong by assuming that art would have an essence, and he discussed art in terms of family resemblance. This anti-essentialist turn, together with the novel understanding of the history of the term and the institution, which showed that what we called art was a historical coincidence, pushed philosophers and theorists out from the earlier situation, where art had appeared as something natural, and something that rewarded easy definitions. Arthur Danto's "Artworld" (1964) offers a great view on one scene and now, later, idea historically on its groundbreaking, dominant role in the philosophy and theory of art. As a result of global power-relations and the incredible cultural impact of the city, everybody knows something about the New York scene, and following that, what happens in New York does not stay in New York. Although it would be great to shift attention from the dominant centers of the West to other scenes, one can hardly think about a better way to bring people together than by discussing the most famous and central scene of them all, which Danto presented as *the* scene, in a way representing the whole world and its artworlds or art scenes, without any reflection on its role in relationship to other scenes. As there are even famous texts in aesthetics that comment on the New York scene, we hope that the readers can forgive us for this choice, as the focus is on the city's past. We hope to make up for this by introducing many thoughts on scenes in less central cultural centers later on. We do not choose the situation where art scenes like Berlin, New York, Tokyo, London, and Paris have a key role in the formation of how all art scenes thrive.

"The Artworld" (1964)[2] is a study of the inherent logic of the world of art, to be precise, late modern and early contemporary visual art. Danto's basic claim is that the history of art and the theoretical atmosphere of the artworld is the framework for what can be seen as plausible, interesting, and rewarding. It makes change possible and explains why it suddenly felt natural for both Andy Warhol to exhibit *The Brillo Box* and for his Fifth Avenue crowd to experience it in a rewarding way. In his book *Andy Warhol* (2009), Danto recalls that by the 1960s

> America had, for the first time in history, produced world class art through the paintings of the so-called New York School – the great Abstract Expressionist canvases produced during and after World War II. In American art circles, it came as a shock that the Pop artists should repudiate this immense aesthetic achievement, and paint what looked like simpleminded pictures of soup cans or Donald Duck.[3]

Danto himself does not really show that much interest in discussing other scenes or what role scenes themselves could have. Rather, in another article "Works of Art and Mere Real Things" (Danto 1981), he says that Warhol's work would not have been accepted in quattrocento Florence.[4] Could this be read as a claim that there was a scene in fifteenth-century Florence? We do not think this is what he wanted to say. Danto's way of thinking (this also applies to his followers, such as George Dickie, who came up with the institutional theory of art) takes up no questions about when the cultural issue, an artworld where theory and history make things possible, started; although one can extract, that the oldest example he discusses in his work in this respect seems to be (Parisian) impressionism.

Lisa Tickner has, in her otherwise not that theoretical book *London's New Scene: Art and Culture in the 1960s* (2020), a take on artworlds and art scenes. Referring to Lawrence Alloway's essay "The Artworld Described as a System" (1972), Tickner discusses the way the artworld as a concept has been used since the late nineteenth century and the way scene as a concept "seems to have derived from black American jazz slang of the 1940s and 50s." According to Tickner, the difference is not always clear-cut, but she accentuates that artworld as a concept is somehow "all-embracing and self-sufficient" where instead "a 'scene' is open-ended and provisional." She also mentions Alan Solomon's conception of "new art" in post-war New York, and the way Solomon focused on the lively scene which was external to (Tickner here quoting Solomon's) "cultural centres," and without rules and compromises, in a territory where "all the right people turn out for the openings: the exhibitionists, the savants, the chic, the curious, the leaders and the followers, the chicks and the studs,"[5] which, of course, sounds really like New York of the 1960s. In Moscow or Tokyo, the list of friends of art and 'freaks' would have been different. Or, to take a historical route: Alloway writes that "(i)n 1910 Apollinaire described attendance at the opening of the annual exhibition of the Société des Artsten Français: "lovely ladies, handsome gentlemen, academics, generals, painters, models, bourgeois, men of letters, and blue stockings.""[6] Anyway, concentrating on the part of the art sphere where 'the sparks fly' might be useful when one desires to focus on the everyday life of art in process, but theoretically it is not a very good model to think about scenes, as all these margins and places of events are still very much connected to also mainstream institutions. It might be more useful to concentrate micro-geographically on cities and their scenes as wholes. And, not everywhere and not in every moment probably in New York neither is there really a clash between the institutions and the living scene. The interesting thing and the one that makes it harder to grab what scenes are about, vice versa takes on muse-ums and legitimate art centers that theories like Dickie's institutional theory (discussed below), is, of course, the way both publics and 'counterpublics' are in a way always self-organized, as Michael Warner has noted[7].

In his 1951 *The Social History of Art* (Vol 1), Arnold Hauser writes that after flat paleolithic naturalism, which was still mostly about spiritual beings, art developed into something more realistic, and in the end mercantile and bourgeois, and that the history of modernism and later the historical avant-garde starts to distance itself from the mainstream of art (our expression) in this last phase.[8] Of course, we also find the beginning of the philosophical 'games' played out in the leading art scenes that were probably at least some-times just due to the desire to drop out the bourgeois, who were seeking easier pleasures and who had no access to how to decode the most philosophical margins of the art scene.

Although there is much to learn from the institutional debate of the philosophers of the late twentieth century, in a sense, reading Dickie is not very helpful for understanding scenes. The same applies to Bourdieu. Bourdieu might be witty in his critical analysis of the French bourgeois and their appreciation and appropriation of art, but he does not touch at all upon what happens in art, only the world of the people who buy it to achieve status.[9]

While trying to explain how it works when someone puts a work of art for presentation in a museum, and how it then gets appreciated and accepted perhaps by a key member of the (here one could say) scene, Dickie places too much weight on the official art scene, as the works that enter museums are already legitimate at that point. He writes weirdly about 'official art' of the institutions. Dickie's influential thoughts on how the upper-level institu-tional world of artworks with its games of legitimation and approval are best expressed in his *Art and the Aesthetic: An Institutional Analysis* (1974). In *The Art Circle: A Theory of Art* (1984), he comes quite close to crossing the line to discussing art scenes, as he takes up the professional life of the artist, writing that sometimes artists do not really try to reach a broader audience with their work. Here one could have been thinking about the possibility to communicate it to a small community, or a scene, but Dickie chooses to think of a "romantic solitude" vis-á-vis museums.[10] And there are no notes about geographical sites, place, i.e. scenes.

Danto stresses the potential of historicism against essentialism, but one can take the site-specific nature of the work of one of his favorite examples, Robert Rauschenberg, to lead us more into the local nature of New York art.

Danto emphasizes that Rauschenberg could not have erased a de Kooning painting (1953) and then exhibited a stuffed angora goat with an inflated tire (1959, part of the series *Monogram* 1955–1959) earlier or in another historical situation, but he doesn't point out that it wouldn't have been possible in the same era in Moscow, Cologne, Berlin, or Tokyo. And he does not note that Warhol would not have faced the same fertile ground (of the scene) with *The Brillo Box* (1964) or, more broadly speaking, with his revolutionary Fifth Avenue (Stable Gallery) exhibition *The Shop* (same year) in Mumbai or Istanbul, as this was only possible and plausible in New York, at least in one part of its art scene. Danto does not possess geographical sensitivity. Although all major scenes have some kind of connection to the major paradigms in art, they also differ in their own local stories, dynamics, and socio-economic and political contexts.

New York was different, and Warhol's art was born in a fertile atmosphere for it, and although Danto doesn't point out that he discusses the logic of only one scene (he discusses the 'historical' situation), one can see it:

Pop art was part of the cracking of the spirit of Modernism, and the beginning of the Postmodern era in which we live. In December 1961, Claes Oldenburg turned a downtown store on the East Side of Manhattan into a place in which he would sell his sculptures made of plaster, chicken wire, and cloth, painted over with household enamel to form crude representations of everyday things – dresses, tights, panties, cake, soda cans, pie, hamburgers, automobile tires. It was more like a general store than an art gallery, and Oldenburg indeed called it "The Store," as if the place of sales and the items for sale constituted an artwork.[11]

In his "Artworld," Danto speaks about the theoretical atmosphere and history of art needed for the autonomous logic of the artworld. These cultural sensitivities and frameworks for interpretation and experience enable the bold, obscure, and (from an ordinary, everyday point of view) plainly weird work done in the artworld. The accent is historical, not site-specific, thinking about geographical scenes, but for sure, Danto would probably not have argued against the thought that different things were possible in different places.

Different scenes support different works of art. If Danto's ideas on theoretical atmosphere and art history are to be taken as true (on a more local level), at least strong scenes in other cities could be different, with slightly different theoretical atmospheres and histories of art, even if they shared much of what the other scenes have. This is what happens in the Oldenburg-Warhol case, quoted above. Danto explored an understanding of how the artworld worked, but we find it interesting that he did not, as a side project, explore the local nature of the history of art, which looks to us like a seductive side path in his texts.

Danto's aim, of course, is quite universal – to talk about conceptual art as a phenomenon, but still, even that has been very different in different scenes. Danto obviously knew this, but if one really thinks about art, which is the phenomenon Danto sought to understand, it easily comes to mind that the differences might also be worthy of philosophical attention, although one must understand that Danto's main point was to come up with a theory of the logic itself, how the logic of the artworld differs from other territories of culture. Examples of the twentieth-century conceptual art scenes which provide a very different framework for art include Moscow conceptualism, which in the 1970s and the 1980s focused on appropriation, using conceptual art to subvert socialist ideology, and the Cologne art scene (visual conceptual objects). Art scenes are different from each other. Even if the basic logic of them is what Danto wrote about, this makes different things possible in different scenes. Not all the works that are or were viewed as remarkable in one scene become something that the global community would note and respect, like the work of Rauschenberg, but still if one is in deep one scene of contemporary art, it cannot be that hard, we think, to reach an understanding of what happens and what is possible in others.

Returning to New York, even if one could say, on a meta-level, that there are really no formal rules or restrictions that would apply to contemporary art, we would still have the need for an older shop (Oldenburg's) to get to Warhol, the scene supporting a certain type of work, and this is Danto's insight on the locality of a scene (which he also accentuated later, when he wrote that Jeff Koons's work was built on the logic of the art scene of New York[12]). As one can just guess that Oldenburg's work made it possible for Warhol to make his *Shop* easily digestible, why not elaborate on this point about the local nature of this history of art?

We need to think about the history of the scenes. As logically as Oldenburg leads to Warhol (and then eventually to Jeff Koons), the impressionists led to cubism and other isms in Paris – and, of course, when distributed and accepted more globally, they had and still have an impact on every scene. Scenes share a lot, but they are also distinctive. And it is clear that the interconnected nature of the especially strong and impactful big scenes provides us with an idea of what art is globally. It is just that we want to underline the scene as one possible theoretical perspective of thinking about art, and to recall the enormous variety of scenes.

Maybe we should be looking for the global impact of some scenes (Warhol's work had a global impact) and not a monolith when we think of the concept artworld? Danto provided a model but applied it only in a universal manner, not in the global manner that would have been appropriate. So, to understand what the artworld is, should we also study many individual scenes, especially the impactful ones?

Susan Sontag's "Notes on Camp"[13] was published in the same year as Danto's text. If Danto's "artworld" juxtaposed art and popular culture philosophically in its focus on pop art, so did Sontag's camp, a highbrowed way of appropriating mass culture and kitsch through a higher stage of reflection. Sontag, unlike Danto, is quite explicit about targeting a peculiar scene in her article, and although she too speaks about a phenomenon that has global extensions, at the time when she wrote the text, camp was an aesthetic sensibility which was not that well known outside New York – at least by its name, although, for sure, sensibilities like that have existed here and there. She stresses that camp differs in different contexts, and so it is easier for us to read her very American and very much (upper class) New York-based list of typical objects of camp, like "Tiffany lamps" and "scopitone films." All in all, from an East European point of view (ours), the list and many of Sontag's examples look like New York's bourgeois or mainstream popular culture, not something we'd associate with camp (Schoedsack's *King Kong,* the Cuban pop singer, La Lupe), as for us, camp connects more to bad sci-fi and really banal objects. But, of course, even the concept itself has traveled not just in time but to become a global concept, and to be applied differently in different places. In any case, in 1964, New York, the city where camp became mainstream, must have been overwhelmingly into camp, as choreographer Yvonne Rainer included it in the 1964 *No Manifesto,* which listed all the features a dance performance was *not* to include ("No to camp").[14]

Why does Danto not take into account the possibility of thinking about Warhol as camp? This shows how reading texts as part of a certain scene at a certain time makes sense. Sontag compares camp to pop art by saying that pop art is flatter, drier and more serious than camp.[15] From today's perspective, it seems relevant to ask about the relationship of pop art and camp at that time in New York. We could easily read camp elements into Warhol's work, but even if this would not have been obvious, one can see that the scene might have been divided in some sense, as Danto has not even given this a thought. Did Danto not like the camp discussion?

Ultimately, Sontag's article is more sensitive to the local nature of the phenomenon (a "sensibility") she writes about. The text could even be read as a tribute to the avant-garde scene in New York, and the way it appropriates popular culture, or maybe something that at the time would have been called middlebrow culture. Sontag does not universalize her remarks like Danto. When Danto suggests that he has found the philosopher's stone for forging together the entire world's artworlds, Sontag writes about local clubs and other sites, for 'us,' which for her must have meant a community of East Coast American intellectuals and scholars in humanities reading *The Partisan Review,* where the essay was originally published, in a handful of distinguished scenes.

She keeps her discourse narrow and self-reflective scene-wise. Manhattan, or even New York, is not the whole world.

Looking at the history of discourse that is scene-oriented, there are hints here and there that come together with urban development. It appears that scenes are something that at least in the way we use the word today connect more to the European or more broadly the Western cultural system, and it's ideals on freedom, lifestyle and counter culture. Also, Central and Continental Europe was the only area in the world where a distinctive art system developed.[16] Perhaps then it is not that odd to find notes on something we could call scene thinking in the classics of this area. One could, of course, accentuate, like Akira Amagasaki, that in Japan there was something resembling an artworld in the eleventh century. Amagasaki might be extending the concept far beyond the interests of Danto and most contemporaries, but his description of the Japanese cultural system, where artists both taught art to the children of rich families and lived in the red light districts together with outlaws (another version of an early artworld is a network of people who included Zen thinking in their practices, like poets or tea masters), is something that comes close to the idea in some sense, just without the freedom and the free lifestyle, movements, and critical culture that the scenes are about when we discuss them today.[17] We might even want to think that professionalism, the way our work is divided and structured in the contemporary and the modern world, is a key to understanding the situation. If glass-makers in Murano in Venice had a job and they could not really choose what to do (to the extent that some of them fled to Prague in the early modern period), or if authors and painters and musicians in eleventh-century Kashmir, where there was something close to a scene as well, were always subordinated to religion,[18] the European, then more broadly, the Western, and ultimately global scenes are about freedom for artists and their work, also freedom to not sell, to revolt against political powers and to form autonomic culture.

When did scenes appear on the European cultural map, when we think of them as local worlds of art and culture? What makes the stories of Westwood and Jakobson interesting is the combination of intensive urban milieu, intellectual and artistic resources, and the way certain things can happen in a certain kind of place, in a certain atmosphere, in a network, part of a broader network, community, and – only one word really describes it – a scene. Sometimes there might be long histories behind these formations that in the end also suit the narratives, where people seek to strengthen local identities, nationalism, and ethnic belonging. But they are not the focus of our aims, and, in fact, they cannot dominate what we are interested in discussing as a scene, which is about people coming together, sharing space, and using it freely. As scenes of something, e.g. painting or experimental music, accentuate belonging to a broader constellation, network, and/or reality, someone might want to use the late 1990s trend concept 'glocal,' which would not be bad as a tag for our discourse, although it is not necessary that this locality is expressed or accentuated, which is typical for the use of this concept.

We will return to details later, but intuitively we feel somewhat uneasy about using the concept of scene for Renaissance Florence, for example. In Michael Baxandall's *Painting & Experience in Fifteenth-Century Italy* (1972), the cultural world of the Florentines, from theater to craft, had explanatory power when the author discusses painting and sculpture,[19] but one could hardly use the word 'scene' about the endeavors of Botticelli and his peers. That was more of a world of craft and professions that were highly administered.

As we write in our article "The Art Scenes" (2018), "A scene is an intensive unit where professionals come together not just in work but also in sharing their everyday activities, and which is therefore something that is possible only in cities. This intensity makes it possible to form autonomic structures for art practice."[20] If we lend our minds to Foucauldian thinking for a moment:

> (W)e are here talking about a variety of discursive formations with articulate properties and character: geographical conditions, traditional artistic production, forms of art, behavior, habits and expectations of the audience, theoretical approaches and specificity of reflections affect arts. For the understanding of a particular art scene and work of art it is necessary to consider and be sensitive to each conceptual formation.[21]

We can only talk about art scenes with the advent of modernism, when civil society began to develop, in which freedom of expression was valued with the appreciation of freedom, the presence of leisure time, and new forms of networking that were typical for the modern age, and even more for our contemporary era. Likewise, the concept of art has been formed in the sense we use it, in certain modifications, even today, as part of this urban development. The history of the concept and institution of art is not about the countryside, and mostly it is run by a handful of cities. Of course, it is not just the concept itself, but mainly the fact that the nature of culture has changed significantly, as a result of new technologies and social and economic changes, which makes it interesting. In the words of Arnold Hauser, "The most striking phenomenon connected with the progress of technology is the development of cultural centers into large cities in the modern sense; these form the soil in which the new art is rooted."[22]

And in these new cities there was a gradual division within the culture, which from the middle of the nineteenth century was beginning to divide into popular culture and so-called high art. As Andreas Huyssen describes it, this "great divide" marked art from several sides, but, in particular, it left a fear of contamination by popular or mass culture.[23] The only salvation was the separation of art from other areas of life, which also resulted in the creation of isolated communities of artists that were increasingly different from the rest of society. Therefore, only then can we talk about the origin of art scenes and the birth of the world of art, which could not exist without scenes. And, as we know, the legitimate artists and entertainers found themselves side by side in the new modern urban environment, as the paintings of the impressionists show.

One illustrative thread starts with Charles Baudelaire and continues with Walter Benjamin. Baudelaire's essays on modern life, dandyism, flaneurs, and modern art can be read through a modernist lens, but he is portraying some kind of an urban cultural scene. Definitely, scenes are urban. Was mid-nineteenth-century Paris the first scene? At least we would not be that far off if we took this as a starting point. There were cafes, and there was artistic, political, and professional freedom. Baudelaire did not only portray the world of the bourgeois. The artists in modernist circles in Paris in the mid-nineteenth century traversed to other areas of the city, partly in search of ideas and inspiration, but also increasingly affordable living as their modern life had made them much poorer after the death of the upper-class artist who still had better patronage in the pre-industrial world, where money was inherited, and the traditional rich had a taste for art and a desire to become immortal through patronage. It was not much later when Picasso and Apollinaire lived in slum-like circumstances in Paris, and the process of translocating artists into the same territories, where they mashed-up with the working class, prostitutes, and the street people, might have been taking its first steps. One could say that the first scene was born through downshifting and gentrification, classes mixing – as Montmartre soon became was lucrative for people, as the fame of its artists grew.

In his text on early modern Paris, Nicholas Hewitt writes

(I)t is possible to talk of a cultural geography in respect of all the great European cities of the nineteenth and twentieth centuries, which enables us to identify those specific urban districts that became centres of cultural activity and production, and those institutions, particularly cafés, that served as regular meeting points for writers and artists.[24]

Besides the cafes and the cheap housing that evolved around universities and publishing houses, Hewitt also discusses the huge number of émigrés, which, of course, is a major feature of all successful art scenes.[25] He says that the contemporary world with its mass media and cinema would be less in need of geographical centers, but anyone who is a member of a scene today would question that. People also travel more than ever to trendy cities to experience their cultural scenes.

Walter Benjamin's unfinished *Arcades Project* (1927–1940) comprises another set of texts, where the roots of the contemporary life form are found. His focus first on Baudelaire's texts on modernity – happening just in the streets, entertainment venues, and cafes looks a lot like a cluster of scene notes, as much as Benjamin's ideas on Berlin and London too. Targeting individual cities, he was chasing the urban modern life form, and recorded different ways of this existence, from London to Paris to Berlin.

Naturally, the role of the scenes comes from this urban change. Today our talk is about the kind of cultural urban formations that Benjamin targeted. We discuss cities – "have you visited Prague, the gallery scene is great" – and their venues, atmospheres, and residences.[26] As we write in our article "The Art Scenes":

> In general, the increased interest in cities and urban culture is central for today's life, the way we travel to cities more than ever, not to mention how many tourist guides and sites there are, and how much they focus on design districts, semi-artistic hipster areas, and townships that have been taken over by artists. Cities even support and develop these areas.[27]

Paris might have been the first life form where artists had a central role in how the nightlife and the pastimes arose, and they themselves – just think about Degas and Renoir – made this evident in their visual appraisals of dancers, bartenders, and prostitutes at Montmartre. What Baudelaire wrote about Paris with its new electrified way of life, radical art expression, and urban identity could not have had, as Benjamin notes, much to do with any other city. We read its key thoughts as grounding words of modernity, modern life and modernism, but what if we turn our gaze to the fact that the notes are very site specific? Modern nightlife developed fast at the time along with the role of the artist, namely the idea of being a starving one[28] and 'free,'[29] and if we believe Benjamin, Berlin had and still has a more openly spatial nature, and London a more industrial, mass (of people)-driven nature (which Edgar Allan Poe described in his short stories).

Everyday mobility has increased to the level that it is easy to not just visit cities, but for professionals to come to grips with many different scenes – a thing that was reserved to very few in the historical modern decades. Benjamin, of course, had the possibility, and so did Westwood and Jakobson at a time when it was slowly probably becoming normal (at least we can say this about Westwood's 1970s and 1980s). In Baudelaire's and Benjamin's texts, things seem to happen in a geographically narrow area, especially when we talk about Paris – and this is typical for scenes; they 'take place' in certain areas. Montmartre was maybe the first in the glorious line of townships like

Camden, Greenwich Village, and Prenzlauer Berg, and even more marginal areas in cities have become scenes on their own, inside the bigger ones. Although the birth of the scenes probably was a very slow process that is hard-to-trace, we can see the whole culture of urbanism showing how cities themselves started producing modern, distinctive cultures. The emergence of art scenes must somehow also be related to the internationalization of the big cities. Göran Therborn calls this "globalized urban nationalism":

> The notion of the 'world city' began to circulate in Europe just before World War I. In Germany, it was used to signal the rise of Berlin as a *Weltstadt*, something more self-evident than Paris and London. In the last third of the nineteenth century, a universal recognition of European 'civilization' and urban splendour began to develop.[30]

The whole issue of scenes cannot, of course, be distinguished from the broader process of urbanization, and the way that big cities have been divided into clearly different sectors and townships, some becoming homes for scenes. Nor can we forget the way modern culture, urban centers at the forefront, developed so that people met increasingly in the same spaces, more democratically, and with fewer social and sexual constraints.

Jürgen Habermas's work on the public sphere,[31] on the way we found places to exchange thoughts and a kind of a cultural space for this exchange (he mentions salons as an early platform for this) could in some sense be thought of as connected to the development of something we call scenes. He writes this about eighteenth-century continental culture: "The "town" was the life center of civil society not only economically; in cultural-political contrast to the court, it designated especially an early public sphere in the world of letters whose institutions were the coffee houses, the *salons*, and the *Tischgesellschaften* (table societies). The heirs of the humanistic-aristocratic society, in their encounter with the bourgeois intellectuals (through sociable discussions that quickly developed into public criticism), built a bridge between the remains of a collapsing form of publicity (the courtly one) and the precursor of a new one: the bourgeois public sphere." This included cafés (a late seventeenth-century addition to culture), and other places alike, where people could exchange ideas and thoughts.[32]

We don't often think about the fact that the way we have spaces where people meet and hang out is very new. There were not even concert halls before the late eighteenth century,[33] café culture began to gather intellectuals in the eighteenth century, and the way that today we have clubs, open galleries, and other joints where people meet, hang-out, exchange thoughts, and also present art is a recent thing in culture. In their work on the development of modernity and urban culture, thinkers like Baudelaire and Benjamin showed us a way to understand the development of scenes, and Paris, with its

Haussmanian open boulevards, probably produced many changes in the way things function (the street became also a scene for showing off and presenting fashion), so, that by Magritte's time, in the late 1920s when he came to Paris, there was a convention and pressure to move to Bohemian areas, which Magritte, as we have discussed, did not follow. But there are also many interesting historical encounters and relocations that show us how deep some of the problems and structures of scenes sit.

Notes

1 For the latter interpretation, see Lawrence Grossberg, *We Gotta Get Outta This Place: Popular Conservativism and Postmodern Culture* (New York: Routledge, 1992).

2 Arthur C. Danto, "The Artworld," *The Journal of Philosophy* 61, no. 19 (1964): 571–584.

3 Arthur C. Danto, *Andy Warhol* (New Haven CT: Yale University Press, 2009), xi.

4 Chapter 1 ("Works of Art and Mere Real Things," 1–32) of Arthur C. Danto's *The Transfiguration of the Commonplace* (1981), is built on this idea, which stems from Heinrich Wölfflin's thought that not everything is possible at every time.

5 Lisa Tickner, *London's New Scene: Art and Culture in the 1960s* (New Haven CT and London: Yale University Press, 2020), see especially pages 17–19 (quote on page 18). See also Lawrence Alloway's "Network: The Art World Described as a System," *Artforum*, September 1972, 28–32. Alloway discusses the way artworks are seen and discussed in studios, before exhibiting, in his essayistic notes on the way the 'art world' functions on different levels and in different contexts. Alan Solomon's book that Tickner quotes is *New York: The New Art Scene* (New York: Leo Castelli Gallery, 1967).

6 In Alloway, "Network."

7 Michael Warner, "Publics and Counterpublics," in *Public Culture* (Durham NC: Duke University Press, 2002), 49–90.

8 Arnold Hauser, *The Social History of Art* (New York: Routledge, 2005).

9 Bourdieu, *Distinctions.*

10 George Dickie, *Art and the Aesthetic: An Institutional Analysis* (Ithaca NY: Cornell University Press, 1974). George Dickie, *The Art Circle: A Theory of Art* (New York: Haven Publications, 1984), see page 65–66 for the note.

11 Danto, *Andy Warhol*, 31.

12 See Danto, Arthur C., Gunnar B. Kvaran, Jeff Koons, Rem Koolhas, and Hans Ulrich Obrist, *Jeff Koons: Retrospektiv/Retrospective* (Oslo: Astrup Fearnley Museet for Moderne Kunst, 2004).

13 Susan Sontag, "Notes on Camp," in *Against Interpretation* (New York: Vintage, 1966), 275–292.

14 Republished on 1000manifestos (www.1000manifestos.com). (The following) link visited April 14, 2023. http://www.1000manifestos.com/yvonne-rainer-no-manifesto/.

15 Sontag, "Notes on Camp," 292.

16 See e.g. Larry Shiner, *The Invention of Art: A Cultural History* (Chicago IL and London: the University of Chicago Press, 2001).

17 Akira Amagasaki, "Art Outside Life and Art as Life," in *Asian Aesthetics*, ed. Ken-ichi Sasaki (Singapore: NUS, 2010).

18 See Ryynänen, *A Philosophy of Central European Art*, Chapter 2.

19 Michael Baxandall, *Painting & Experience in Fifteenth-Century Italy* (Oxford: Oxford University Press, 1972).
20 Jozef Kovalcik and Max Ryynänen, "The Art Scenes," *Contemporary Aesthetics*, Vol 16, 2018. Link: https://digitalcommons.risd.edu/liberalarts_contempaesthetics/vol14/iss1/16/.
21 Ibid.
22 Hauser, Arnold, *The Social History of Art (vol. 4)* (London and New York: Routledge, 2005), 111.
23 Huyssen, Andreas, *After the Great Divide: Modernism, Mass Culture, Postmodernism* (Bloomington: Indiana University Press, 1986), vii–xii.
24 Nicholas Hewitt, "Shifting Cultural Centres in Twentieth-century Paris," in *Parisian Fields*, edited by Michael Sheringham (London: Reaktion Books Ltd, 1996).
25 Ibid.
26 This is one of the topics in Angela McRobbie's book *Be Creative: Making a Living in the New Culture Industries* (Cambridge: Polity, 2016).
27 Kovalcik & Ryynänen, "The Scenes." Good to note here, many classical continental cities have invited scholars to produce books about the art of their city. Vienna, which we often comment on in our book, is one. See e.g. Mario Valeri Manera, *Le arti a Vienna: Dalla seccessione alla caduta dell impero asburgico* (Venice: Edizioni la Biennale, 1984) and Peter Vergo, *Art in Vienna 1898–1918* (New York: Phaidon Press, 1975).
28 See e.g. Naomi Ritter, *Art as Spectacle: Images of Entertainment since Romanticism* (Columbia: University of Missouri Press, 1985).
29 See Carole Talon-Hugon's great idea historical inquiry on art and freedom: Carole Talon-Hugon, *Le conflit des heritages* (Avignon: Actes Sud-Papiers, 2017).
30 Göran Therborn, *Cities of Power.* (London and New York: Verso, 2017), 289–290.
31 We thank Hanno Soans for his comments on Habermas, which opened our eyes for the connection.
32 Jürgen Habermas, *The Structural Transformation of the Public Sphere* (Cambridge MA: MIT Press, 1991), 29. Also David Chaney notes, referring to Habermas, the impact of today's lack of community in the Western world and the way this might affect the formation of cultural networks. See, David Chaney, *The Cultural Turn: Scene Setting Essays on Contemporary Cultural History* (London: Taylor & Francis, 1994), 28, 29.
33 On this late development, see e.g. Shiner, *The Invention of Art*, 192–193.

Bibliography

Alloway, Lawrence. "Network: The Art World Described as a System." *Artforum* 11, No. 1 (September 1972): 28–32.
Amagasaki, Akira. "Art Outside Life and Art as Life." In *Asian Aesthetics*, edited by Ken-ichi Sasaki, 30–40. Singapore: NUS, 2010.
Baxandall, Michael. *Painting & Experience in Fifteenth-Century Italy.* Oxford: Oxford University Press, 1972.
Bourdieu, Pierre. *Distinction.* Translated by Richard Nice. London: Routledge, 1984.
Chaney, David. *The Cultural Turn: Scene Setting Essays on Contemporary Cultural History.* London: Taylor & Francis, 1994.
Danto, Arthur C. "The Artworld." *The Journal of Philosophy* 61, No. 19 (1964): 571–584.
Danto, Arthur C. *The Transfiguration of the Commonplace.* Cambridge MA: Harvard University Press, 1983.

Danto, Arthur C. *Andy Warhol*. New Haven CT: Yale University Press, 2009.

Danto, Arthur C., Gunnar B. Kvaran, Jeff Koons, Rem Koolhas, and Hans Ulrich Obrist. *Jeff Koons: Retrospektiv/Retrospective*. Oslo: Astrup Fearnley Museet for Moderne Kunst, 2004.

Dickie, George. *Art and the Aesthetic: An Institutional Analysis*. Ithaca NY: Cornell University Press, 1974.

Dickie, George. *The Art Circle: A Theory of Art*. New York: Haven Publications, 1984.

Grossberg, Lawrence. *We Gotta Get Outta This Place: Popular Conservativism and Postmodern Culture*. New York: Routledge, 1992.

Habermas, Jürgen. *The Structural Transformation of the Public Sphere*. Translated by Thomas Burger. Cambridge MA: MIT Press, 1991.

Hauser, Arnold. *The Social History of Art*, Vol. 4. New York: Routledge, 2005.

Hewitt, Nicholas. "Shifting Cultural Centres in Twentieth-century Paris." In *Parisian Fields*, edited by Michael Sheringham, 30–45. London: Reaktion Books Ltd, 1996.

Huyssen, Andreas. *After the Great Divide: Modernism, Mass Culture, Postmodernism*. Bloomington: Indiana University Press, 1986.

Kovalcik, Jozef and Max Ryynänen. "The Art Scenes." *Contemporary Aesthetics* 16 (2018). https://contempaesthetics.org/newvolume/pages/article.php?articleID=847.

Manera, Mario Valeri, ed., *Le arti a Vienna: Dalla seccessione alla caduta dell impero asburgico*. Venice: Edizioni la Biennale, 1984.

McRobbie, Angela. *Be Creative: Making a Living in the New Culture Industries*. Cambridge: Polity, 2016.

Ritter, Naomi. *Art as Spectacle: Images of Entertainment since Romanticism*. Columbia: University of Missouri Press, 1985.

Ryynänen, Max. *On the Philosophy of Central European Art: The History of an Institution and Its Global Competitors*. Lanham MD: Lexington Books, 2020.

Shiner, Larry. *The Invention of Art: A Cultural History*. Chicago IL and London: The University of Chicago Press, 2001.

Solomon, Alan. *New York: The New Art Scene*. New York: Leo Castelly Gallery, 1967.

Sontag, Susan. "Notes on Camp." In *Against Interpretation*, 275–292. New York: Vintage, 1966.

Talon-Hugon, Carole. *Le conflit des heritages*. Avignon: Actes Sud-Papiers, 2017.

Therborn, Göran. *Cities of Power*. London, New York: Verso, 2017.

Tickner, Lisa. *London's New Scene: Art and Culture in the 1960s*. New Haven CT and London: Yale University Press, 2020.

Vergo, Peter. *Art in Vienna 1898–1918*. New York: Phaidon Press, 1975.

Warner, Michael. "Publics and Counterpublics." In *Public Culture*. Durham NC: Duke University Press, 2002.

4   If Beale Street Could Talk Like Greenwich Village

Scenes, Class, Ethnicity, and Some Notes on Contemporary Urban Studies through Scenes

In Istanbul, a Western traveler can become surprised at the way all carpet shops seem to be on the same street – and then, when looking for clothes, you must pick another street. On the other hand, this is the way art scenes work, too, although usually you don't sell art on just one street. You walk on 5th Avenue, and every gallery, in the end, sells (or just exhibits) the same kind of stuff, and with small variants the same kind of exhibiting activity happens in Prenzlauer Berg and was already commonplace in Soho a long time ago. Art picks up in only certain parts of the cities. In big cities, there are many areas where art happens.

Sometimes street culture develops in this way, too. It places its goods intensively only in one area. The Hush Rap History Bus takes tourists from Manhattan over the Macombs Dam Bridge to the original sites where rap and hip-hop developed in The Bronx and then Harlem. From Kool Herc's house at 1520 Sedgwick Avenue, where the legendary block party organized by his sister (to get money for new clothes) was organized August 13, 1973, and from where scratching and rapping really took a strong step forward culturally, the bus takes the tourist through the Graffiti Wall of Fame in Spanish Harlem, through a chain of clubs and studios where pre-rappers like James Brown and early rap groups like the Crash Crew made their fame. A visitor who knows about the incredible global impact of hip-hop and who has maybe already witnessed the huge size of New York is in awe: Is the original area that for years carried this culture actually, really, so small?

When one of us asked an art dealer why he planned to open his gallery on a street where there were six other galleries, he said: "It is easier for people interested in painting to find me here. Among completely different kind of stores – for example, selling vegetables and clothes – my gallery would be lost." If galleries were located all over the city, it would also be more difficult to visit them.

The African American writer James Baldwin (1924–1987) grew up in Harlem, which, like The Bronx later, might at the time of Baldwin's youth have been quite a place, thinking about the music scene, without forgetting the artistic Harlem Renaissance, which spanned from the late 1910s until

DOI: 10.4324/9781003412786-5

the mid-1930s, and extended culturally from literature (Langston Hughes, Alice Dunbar Nelson) and music (Fats Waller, Bessie Smith, Billie Holiday, Benny Goodman, Jelly Roll Morton, Louis Armstrong), and the visual arts (Archibald J. Motley, Augusta Savage) to philosophy (Alain Locke) – and for sure left strong traces. All this happened in a very small geographical area. As we are talking about an ethnic margin and their site in the city, it probably developed even more strongly locally than the white middle-class art scenes. Still, one should not forget that the movement did not in the end remain just local but had its "franchises" all the way to Paris. In the Harlem area, that had become African American in the early 1900s, great African American migrations occurred, especially in the 1920s, to make the township a special one in New York. With its sites and places like the Cotton Club, and journals like *Opportunity: Journal of Negro Life*, Harlem, with all its extensions to other black communities at the time, was probably very much a scene of its own.

Interestingly, when Baldwin wrote about his early life, he claimed that when he was 15, and met the painter Beauford Delaney in the Lower Manhattan Greenwich Village – the white art scene of the time with its beat movements, New York University, and New School – he learned from him the idea that he too (or any black person) could become an "artist."[1] It might have been that Harlem was still less of an "art" scene without artist identities (these cultural functions had developed since the Renaissance geographically broadly speaking in Central, Continental, and Southern Europe[2]) and ideas of "authorship",[3] and that Baldwin's interests might have been a bit different from the post-renaissance of Harlem's culture, so he needed an external person's help to reach his prime on the path he had chosen. On the other hand, as art as a system of identity, authorship, agency, and institution was from the beginning a Continental European upper-class invention, it could be that one really, in the end, had to travel the geographically small but culturally long road from Harlem to Greenwich Village to make it into the 'art system' – and, of course, if one wanted to reach broader audiences, the power-center of the dominantly white middle-class art scene, which was built on (again, broadly speaking) Central and Continental European enlightenment and modernist ideals, was probably the only opportunity for that.

Baldwin later left even New York and settled in Paris when he was 24 years old. He fought against the idea of being a "negro writer," and the way people of color still today fight prejudices in the artworld tells a lot about the way its ethnically European upper-class origins still have an effect on scenes (besides other everyday prejudices). Baldwin's *If Beale Street Could Talk* (1974) tells the story of a poor couple, of which the husband, a sculptor, becomes wrongly accused of rape and enters the systematically racist incarceration system of America, and it both humanized African Americans and gave a voice to Harlem.

How come the Harlem Renaissance was not able to build an alternative form of a permanent scene? Is the original idea of art, the European one, so much better institutionally backed up? How come haven't we been able to build more inclusive art and culture scenes is another question – which should be raised everywhere, although art scenes are changing. How come, in big cities, can so many and so different scenes live side by side so well, and how come we haven't had much discussion about this cultural and urban phenomenon?

Whatever, we talk about cities nearly always when we talk about scenes, and, as we have already noted in our earlier examples, changing city means a lot. Baldwin's case shows a fantastic example of changing class-wise and ethnically the scene in one big city – in middle-sized cities this is hardly possible and in small cities almost not at all – but what is truly remarkable, in his case, is, still, not the voyage to Paris, which in the end was probably quite like New York, but the way Baldwin landed in Istanbul. He arrived there 1961 and knocked on the door of Engin Cezzar, a Turkish actor he had met in New York in 1958. The original plan was to reach Africa, but according to Baldwin himself, he lacked the energy and stopped in Turkey – where he in the end spent a major part of the 1960s. There he wrote, for example, *Another Country* (1962), *The Fire Next Time* (1963) and *Tell Me how Long the Train's Been Gone* (1968).

"I find it easier to work here than I do anywhere else," Baldwin claimed, and added that he felt that he was left alone in Istanbul. In the US, his experiences as a black man had been harsh. But Istanbul was more welcoming. He was not harassed by the police. He could enter all restaurants. And, importantly, he was met in friendly manner by the intellectual and artistic scene. The Kurdish Turkish writer and human rights activist Yaşar Kemal, famous, for example, for his novel *Mehmed, My Hawk* (1955), besides speaking a lot about the oppression of the Kurdish people, became one of Baldwin's friends. He also spoke at length about racism in Turkey. He said about being black that "[w]e don't have that category," that "[t]here are only people with darker skins."[4] In Istanbul, Baldwin's moniker was "Arap" (Arab). Kemal, who himself had come from a village in the Eastern Provinces (his village had paid for his university education), had made Istanbul his scene.

It is hard for us as authors to imagine what it meant to come from close to the Iraqi border, from a small village where people do not have education, and where ideals stemming from Florence, Paris, and Berlin do not have a strong impact, to a center like Istanbul, which today has 16 million inhabitants. But, of course, even coming to a place where there are cafés and café life is already to some extent a step toward the scenes. The French Parisian scene of the Enlightenment already worked in cafés. The art scene consists of artists whose favorite places, style of dress, and taste define the nature of the scene. They work out their own cultural reality. Build it themselves. And they need to meet in places, like cafés and bars where to read and write together, where to land after openings and premieres. Without them, institutions would be just desperate presentation spaces not so different from shopping malls.

And cafés everywhere are famous for the artists who sat there and wrote. They did not have working places and they needed to get away from home, so here the writers might really have had a special role.

Sarah Bakewell describes neatly the situation in Paris in the mid-twentieth century, when the character of the (existentialist) art scene was highly influenced by Jean Paul Sartre and Simon de Beauvoir, while cafes became the epicenter of intellectual life:

> Sartre and Beauvoir spent many years living in the cheap Saint-Germain hotels and writing all day in cafés, mainly because these were wormer places to go then the unheated hotel rooms. (...) Sartre enjoyed working in public spaces amid noise and bustle. He and Beauvoir held court with friends, colleagues, artists, writers, students and lovers, all talking at once and bound by ribbons of cigarette or pipe smoke.[5]

Although these places have later on become tourist attractions, and their idealization might be kitschy, they have really had a very practical role in shaping art scenes.

The origin and true nature of the social status of the members of the scene may not be evident. Bourdieu describes many specifics of the functioning of the French artistic environment, which is, at least through selected "élite" artists, connected to political and economic elites. Most people in highbrow art scenes at least are from the middle class (especially when we talk about classical music), but the situation is different in many alternative art scenes and popular culture scenes.

The fact that we link the art scene and the middle class (without forgetting the ethnicity that Baldwin's story raises as a topic) undoubtedly has its justification and compelling reason. After all, people in art scenes (now talking narrowly without popular culture) are mostly educated, cultured, and culturally confident people. Discussing today's position of intellectuals, John Frow points out that the connection to the middle class in less socially stratified societies does not have to be strong and it is no longer necessary to associate it with the dominant forces of society:

> This is so in particular because of the mediation of two cultural institutions: that of the mass media, which construct heterogeneous global audience rather than class-specific audience; and that of the mass education system, which rather than being directly tied to the reproduction of an élite, now has the more diffuse function of the differential formation of cultural capital.[6]

As Angela McRobbie points out, the democratization of the arts has brought to the art scene to a much greater extent people from the lowest social classes who have brought in their themes, values, and often tastes.[7] We are aware that each art scene in this respect deserves its own class analysis, which can reveal its structure, values, and connection to the rest of society. Doing this is, though, out of the scope of this book, and would require field work. However, what we consider necessary to emphasize in this respect is that entering the art scene for those who come from the working class of society is a fundamental change in their position within society. Annie Ernaux describes this experience of "conquering" culture and art very precisely in the books *La Place* or *Une Femme*, as does Didier Eribon in *Returning to Rheims*. For them, culture and art are tools of emancipation, but also means of defining oneself against one's origins. Both consistently state the boundaries that each had to advance in order to become part of the art scene. Eribon presents a description of this inner formation:

> An interest in art is something that is learned. I learned it. It was part of my project of nearly complete self-reeducation, necessary in order to move into a different world, a different class—and to put some distance between myself and the world and the class from which I came.[8]

This transformation of oneself had to be completed by everyone who entered the scene and was not part of it from the very beginning. For those who are insiders and are part of the art scene because of their origins, the line between the world and art is invisible. As Eribon points out, these children from better families do not have the feeling of belonging to a certain social class. Unlike those who come from the working class, who are constantly aware of their origin, they don't need to thematize it at all, because they don't realize at all that they are privileged, just like "people in a dominant class position do not notice that they are positioned, situated, within a specific world (just as someone who is white isn't necessarily aware of being that)."[9]

What Eribon states in a broader social sense we can also apply to the art scene. Many artists are so closed into them that many times it seems as if the world does not even exist outside the scene. They do not understand that those who do not belong to their microcosm often have completely different priorities, believe in radically different values and have their life goals formulated in a completely different manner. Perhaps the only thing that really bothers them is that they don't understand why not everyone is part of their scene. Maybe that's why many of them take it as their mission to convince these ignorant people of the beauty of their universe, or at least to present their incomprehensible world to them in the hope that they will at least touch their emotions a little.

Eribon succeeded in the fight to enter the art scene, but often it may not succeed at all. The fact that this world can in a sense also be an impregnable world is stated by Annie Ernaux in connection with her mother, who all her life wanted to belong to a higher, cultural society, or even artistic circles. She didn't make it, but she didn't stop trying. However, when she was close, she could not take the next step. She kept doing everything to keep herself out of it, even though she wanted to get in. She preferred physical work because then she felt she was doing something really valuable, as opposed to reading, which was more like killing time. She never crossed the line between everyday life and the "world of art," although she eventually got there, thanks to Ernaux herself, who made her the character of her book, as she herself points out:

> Naturally, this isn't a biography, neither is it a novel, maybe a cross between literature, sociology, and history. It was only when my mother— born in an oppressed world from which she wanted to escape—became story that I started to feel less alone and out of place in a world ruled by words and ideas, the world where she had wanted me to live.[10]

In later books, which also have many elements of autobiography, Ernaux actually describes how she adopted middle-class values and gradually became part of the scene without forgetting where she is coming from. Her novel *Les Années* could be summarized as slow and detailed description of this transformation – from the fearful and anxious girl from the working class with too big respect for art to the self-confident woman who controls her life and has a great reputation at the art scene and even artworld.

Like Didier Eribon, Baldwin also wrestled with his homosexual identity, and like Eribon's, Baldwin's story mostly accentuates homosexuality, also, of course, race – and the class distinction somehow stays overshadowed. Eribon's way of taking up the other story of his life is something that is, of course, easier in Baldwin's case. If *Returning to Rheims* is about remembering working-class life and poverty, and also culture and the need to rethink it loudly, class has somewhat more been a part of black critical discourse right from the beginning, with an intuition about the intersectional nature of the problems, of course, that gained this code word through Kimberlé Crenshaw's groundbreaking work in 1989.[11] Anyway, both tell a story of scenes, one (Baldwin) parting from an infamous one to a famous and legitimate one, and the other (Eribon) leaving a place he did not think of as a scene, but which we could reconstruct to be something alike in a social, class-driven sense, ending up in the upper and middle-class French intellectual scene of Paris, later returning to oblivion, where he had buried his poverty and cultural background. Scenes often make people forget where they are from. They become new homes. Like religious societies, they hide people who have left a past behind them. The structures of scenes are so strong that one can stay in them like one can stay for years in an Ashram or a cult living on a farm.

Notes

1 James Baldwin, *The Price of the Ticket: Collected Nonfiction, 1948–1985* (New York: St Martin's Press, 1985), ix.
2 For the history of art institutions with this accent, see e.g. Max Ryynänen, *On the Philosophy of Central European Art: The History of an Institution and Its Global Competitors* (Lanham MD: Lexington Books, 2020).
3 We here refer to the way the idea of authorship developed in continental Europe and became a trademark of the art system. See e.g. Martha Woodmansee, *The Author, Art, and the Market: Rereading the History of Aesthetics* (New York: Columbia University Press, 1994).
4 Quoted in *"Importance of Elsewhere"* an article for *NUAE* by Suzy Hansen: July 3, 2009. https://www.thenationalnews.com/uae/importance-of-elsewhere-1.547108.
5 Sarah Bakewell, *At the Existentialist Café* (London: Penguin Random House, 2016), 12.
6 John Frow, *Cultural Studies and Cultural Value* (Oxford and New York: Clarendon Press and Oxford University Press, 1995), 86.
7 This is one of the main currents in McRobbie, *Be Creative*.
8 Didier Eribon, *Returning to Reims* (Los Angeles CA: Semiotext(e), 2013), 106.
9 Ibid., 70.
10 The original: Annie Ernaux, *Une Femme* (Paris: Gallimard, 1987), 106. The quote: Annie Ernaux, *A Woman's Story*, translated by Tanya Leslie (New York: Seven Stories Press, 1991), 91.
11 Kimberlé Crenshaw, "Demarginalizing the Intersection of Race and Sex: A Black Feminist Critique of Antidiscrimination Doctrine, Feminist Theory and Antiracist Politics," *University of Chicago Legal Forum* 1 (1989): 139–167.

Bibliography

Bakewell, Sarah. *At the Existentialist Café*. London: Penguin Random House, 2016.
Baldwin, James. *The Price of the Ticket: Collected Nonfiction, 1948–1985*. New York: St Martin's Press, 1985.
Crenshaw, Kimberlé. "Demarginalizing the Intersection of Race and Sex: A Black Feminist Critique of Antidiscrimination Doctrine, Feminist Theory and Antiracist Politics." *University of Chicago Legal Forum* 1 (1989): 139–167.
Eribon, Didier. *Returning to Reims*. Translated by Michael Lucey. Los Angeles CA: Semiotext(e), 2013.
Ernaux, Annie. *Une Femme*. Paris: Gallimard, 1987.
Ernaux, Annie. *A Woman's Story*. Translated by Tanya Leslie. New York: Seven Stories Press, 1991.
Ernaux, Annie. *Les Années*. Paris: Gallimard, 2008.
Frow, John. *Cultural Studies and Cultural Value*. Oxford and New York: Clarendon Press and Oxford University Press, 1995.
McRobbie, Angela. *Be Creative: Making a Living in the New Culture Industries*. Cambridge: Polity, 2016.
Ryynänen, Max. *On the Philosophy of Central European Art: The History of an Institution and Its Global Competitors*. Lanham MD: Lexington Books, 2020.
Woodmansee, Martha. *The Author, Art, and the Market: Rereading the History of Aesthetics*. New York: Columbia University Press, 1994.

5 Aesthetics of the Scenes

We are accustomed to think that the culture which surrounds us creates a certain more or less comforting order of things, where things feel meaningful and logical. These cultural surroundings guide us through our life. And there cultures merge – ethnic, organizational ones, and the ones associated with cultural production.

These contexts warm up the world for us, program, for example, Finns to heat up their sauna on Saturday, and because of cultural conditioning people all around the world react differently to spices, humor, and colors. Partly on this we base our understanding of differing values, ways of experiencing, and atmospheres that exist in this world. Maybe most discussions take national states or languages too much for granted as a base for what can be talked about as cultures, but the idea that we are conditioned, and that this conditioning extends deep in us, is bought by everyone today.

We'd like to add here something that is less-discussed in this context, i.e. cities. Cities really are like small cultures – and definitely they are in many ways often more compact and holistically interwoven than national states, that are so often referred to as cultures ("culture of Italy," "Chinese culture" – just to name two countries where people some time ago could not even speak to each other). Cities work in diverse ways as cultural platforms. Scenes are an important part of that dynamic.

The arts are a special case in culture, whether viewed narrowly, based on legacy of "fine art," or more broadly, then including popular culture, folk culture, and other formations where artistic activity in one way or another is central. Nations and languages dominate ideas on art, too, and too much, of course – as national states (and people striving for independence; think of Sibelius's *Finlandia*, which was composed during the Russian occupation) have been, through museums, cultural institutes, and research, marking their own arts as part of national identity. Although nations and languages have a huge impact on art, it is important to ask the question whether this impact is still overaccentuated.

What is the role of scenes for art, in the end? And, here we raise an aesthetic and philosophical question. We have already studied some traces in

DOI: 10.4324/9781003412786-6

the history of the development of scenes and gone through brief sketches of taxonomical structures and other features of scenes. At this point, we could say that we already know what they are about, mainly. But the last thing needs still to be done: the analysis of their aesthetics, aesthetics in the sense that one could really form new thinking about their role in constituting art itself, not just giving some artistic functions and modes a bigger or lesser part in the scene. What is their aesthetic impact – and could it be larger than that of nations? Cities really offer us tightly interwoven art scenes, which nations cannot, as too-big units, do. It is understandable, that as national thinking became one of the key aspects of Western identity through German philosophers of the nineteenth century, and that nations have worked hard to provide their citizens an idea of a shared culture where many more narrowly local phenomena are presented as national ones, people have adopted a way of thinking about cultures as national cultures – on the side of the view of thinking ethnically, for example, discussing "Arab culture." But it is as weird that we don't have a discussion about cultures in cities or even more in their art and cultural (and intellectual) scenes. We discuss organizational cultures in companies, but we don't think of scenes as cultural formats that could be theorized.

It is simple at this point to note that if countries are not very free, scenes do not work freely or in the same way as they do in freer countries, if they work at all. Totalitarian countries often have only, in some sense, underground scenes, as scenes require a certain amount of freedom, not just freedom for testing out artistic ideas, but for discussion, getting together, and critique. We have read a lot about cultural scenes in the Soviet Union, for example, and how they were both underground and, on the other hand, official.

Through thinking about totalitarian countries, we can better understand how important freedom of expression is for the scenes. In the eighties, before the fall of the Iron Curtain, one could see Central and Eastern European countries striving for this type of freedom, but people there had only limited options and possibilities to work for political change. From today's perspective, it may seem that only the underground movements strove for independence, but, in fact, many official institutions also tried to get into their exhibitions and performances elements of direct or indirect criticism of the regime or the existing social conditions. The underground and the official institutions worked basically for the same change.

Going back to geography, really small countries, like Iceland, are probably not the right places about which to ask whether the city and its scene or the country is one that we should concentrate more on – as the country is so small that it is hard to imagine that there would be anything else than Reykjavik and its extensions all around the island. There are many geopolitical issues to understand.

As we have already written, it does not look plausible that being a member of the London art scene, for instance, would make it hard for one to enter the Mumbai art scene – or the Rome art scene. There is, of course, always something to learn, but the main ways of existing in the scene, and the way the art is done, is somehow already there, a literacy that one gains in a scene. It is like when one has been to one university, it is not that hard to understand how another works – through understanding the way we think of faculties, organize lectures, and do research.

Here we'd like to think that any good scene conditions us to understand other related scenes; i.e. being in the Stockholm poetry scene conditions you to enter the Berlin poetry scene, and even the Tokyo scene to a major extent – as much as language differences allow. In the same way, but on a meta-level, being once in any art scene helps to understand all other art scenes. Poetry slams, bookshops, and writers' cafés are the same in Jakarta and Bogota.

People who have never been in an art scene don't understand how openings and book presentations are and are not "work." They don't understand the way one learns, breathes art in the scene – through discussions, meeting other people, and so on. It is not just about networks. It is about art itself, to some extent. There are people who decide to not be in scenes anymore or never to enter them really, but most of us in scenes need them for our work and our understanding. They are the places where we are constantly educated and refreshed, so that we can be wise and sensitive in what we are doing. They are not a side matter to our practice. They are at the heart of the practice. A Mercedes dealer might have to hang out in social situations outside of official working times, but this networking is not the same. We constantly condition ourselves in the scenes as art is a living practice which keeps reacting to the world and changing with changes in the world – and, of course, the same applies to intellectual circles, too. In the scenes, the artworlds are aesthetically in an endless state of becoming.

It is there where we learn our modes of intentionality for art, phenomenologically speaking. After learning how to do and/or look at, for instance, painting, the currents of change in it, and the variety of things done keep educating us, making us sensible and sensitive all the time. It might have forced us look at political painting 20 years ago, 3D ten years ago – and now we notice that an increasing amount of our colleagues in the field are into quite classical pictorial representation, but with new themes and topics. It is not that we need to know "what is in," and it is not that one could not choose to just stay out and still work in arts or enjoy what one sees in journals and occasionally in museums, but that this is what art and culture in the end is for many of us, art and culture close to us. Our eyes learn again to see things differently – or to warm up old habits, too. We orient our ways of experiencing based on our experiences in the scene. We are conditioned and creative pretty much following their impact, ready to make up new moves and interpretive strategies, whatever the scene asks for – which then, later on, big museums translate for the broader public. Scenes educate differently, give different skills.

How many people "live" in scenes? It is hard to say, but an active city with half a million inhabitants could, we guess, have thousands of scene members (in the arts, broadly speaking), and maybe even tens of thousands who have a small niche or contact which keeps them sometimes included in these cultural spheres.

How do we discuss scenes philosophically? Is there any way we could, for example, try to get into them through classical thinkers – like Martin Heidegger? Could the distinctive cultural nature and potentials of different scenes, even if they are an urban phenomenon, resonate with the work of the major rural philosopher of the twentieth century, Heidegger? In "The Origin of the Work of Art" (1935–1936), he writes:

> It is the temple-work that first joins together and simultaneously gathers around itself the unity of those paths and relations in which birth and death, disaster and blessing, victory and disgrace, endurance and decline obtain the form of destiny for human being. …The temple first gives to things their look and to humanity their outlook on themselves.[1]

Heidegger's life work started in the footsteps of his teacher Edmund Husserl, with quite universalist aspirations. In *Being and Time* (1927), he set out to understand basic elements and grounds of Being through the Dasein analytics he developed[2] and the book is, in principle, for everyone interested in how culture and Being functions. It answers conditioning and how we make sense of the world culturally from a phenomenological point of view. In "The Origin of the Work of Art," the philosopher turned his gaze toward more site-specific issues and art and culture. He narrowed down his interest to local/German issues and side-by-side with that, fantasies on what the Greeks might have been experiencing – which was typical of the Germans of the early twentieth century. While we are not interested in "Germans" (more than "Finns" or "Slovaks"; note the quotation marks, as we don't want to find boundaries for this type of "people"), the idea that cultural conditioning, where art – here Heidegger really goes micro-geographical – has a major role, not just for artists, though, but for a "culture," takes a step already toward the idea of scenes. Heidegger discusses the constitutive nature of being someone in Athens, following the impact of the temple there – and the way artworks have a constitutive role in culture.

In the end, "The Origin of the Work of Art" is not much of an art theory. Heidegger discusses van Gogh's painting of shoes and the Greek temple (of Athene, in Athens), but not as "art" in the (whether now or then) normal sense. He offers another reading of what one could mean with art, one where it has a constitutive nature for culture. He stressed the way art depends "upon its roots in native soil."[3] And he started but soon quit translating Lao Tzu with his Chinese student as he did not believe that a complex work from another culture like the *Tao-Te-Ching* could be translated into German.[4]

We all end up having some kind of a cultural destiny (being thrown into (*Geworfenheit*) a certain cultural situation) and we all have some deep cultural understanding and/or sensitivity, which we feel is hard to share with people with different backgrounds, our cultural reality. Here, Heidegger claims, certain key works are important. The Greek temple functions in his work as an example for the way one work can form the basis of the life of a whole people (The Greeks; *Volk*). Thinking about the people of ancient Athens, maybe not many works were visually, culturally, and ritualistically leading them as people, and Heidegger claims that the temple recollected the destiny, symbols, and the deeper meanings of them. Things are what they are in relation to the Temple. And he wrote about a city. Are some things untranslatable from one cultural scene to another?

Maybe Heidegger felt a need to work out a path beyond the overtly universalist (formalist, surface-driven) tenets of thinking of his time – where the Vienna School of philosophy and the avant-gardists alike worked on universal languages, where the Socialists moved people thousands of miles from their homes to join new factories in Siberia, and where Ford, together with many other pioneers of mechanization, worked out new factory models for work and lifestyle. What goes beyond the universally possible leaned maybe in the end a bit too much on the Germans here, although it is interesting that Heidegger really accentuated increasingly his own Black Forest area in later turns of his thinking, a smaller geographical area.

Analyzing this way of thinking, one could believe that, for example, in some areas of Finland certain experiences of forest and sauna could have this kind of constitutive character, not being good or bad, or productive or not-productive, but if not central, at least in some sense connected to everything else, supporting the whole (although, important to accentuate, again, we do not here want to think that nations or "cultures" (like the Slovaks or the Finns) are monolithic wholes, and this localistic side of Heidegger's thinking is, of course, connected in a complicated manner to the Nationalist Socialist thinking that ruled at the time).

There might not be a reason to buy the story in this sense, but the basic idea of some works building reality and the fact that cultures (one does not have to think national or regional here) gain invisible, own logics and ways of being meaningful is portrayed neatly. Putting aside the "deep level" gained from one's language and being a born member of something, and thinking that some cultural settings are so strong that they can produce own reality, have their own key works that bind them together, and feel maybe even professionally at least having a destiny does not sound in the end like a bad speculation if we look at scenes. Stockholm's film scene might not be what Heidegger wanted to think in the Black Forest or with some ideas of Germanic people, but Ingmar Bergman's films in some sense constitute the sense and imagination of what films are there. Like the temple, Bergman's key films were not just for the film scene, but for all people around – all Swedes, also people talking Swedish or culturally close to his world, for example, in Finland.

A shallowly Heideggerian thinker might ask if this type of strong own reality needs major works, like Bergman's *The Seventh Seal* (1957) or *Wild Strawberries* (1957), that echo the role of the Temple in Heidegger's story, but we do not necessarily see this as something that we should ask. What we want is to just bring forth that the cultural reality and its strength that Heidegger portrays could be something to slightly think about when we gaze at scenes.

In a sense, the whole artworld somehow leans on the visible and invisible traits of beings like Greek temples, Ludwig van Beethoven's *Symphony No. 9 in D minor (Op. 125)* or events like Woodstock.[5] These somehow, of course, constitute what we consider art to be, what we recognize as art and culture, and what warms up our world, and once again we need to think carefully when we are discussing the peculiarity of scenes, when it is about arts and culture all in all. Scenes, though, for sure, have some features that are not as easily sharable, although works can still find productive interpretations in other scenes and the whole broader, even global, art system. And, really, what is interesting about scenes is that they do not necessarily have anything to offer for the local people who do not "inhabit" the scene itself. Heidegger also neatly explains the boundary of understanding something through his example of the temple. It sounds plausible that seeing something remarkable all the time which has an impact on one's ideas on form and aesthetics must condition the inhabitant of a city which contains such a remarkable thing as the Temple of Athene. We cannot say how deep this goes and whether there are aesthetic clashes embedded between people who are conditioned by, for example, an incredible minaret (like Hagia Sophia) or a formally pleasant and socially well-working main library in the center of the city (Oodi, Helsinki, is a good example of this[6]), but for sure, some deep conditioning also happens in the artworld. It is hard to say how much deep conditioning cultures in the end provide us, but yes, if in everyday culture a Nordic person feels relieved and authentic deep in the forest, a Briton might panic when there are only trees around and when there's a long (obscure) way (read: a path, or not even a path) to the next house. The same way an inhabitant of Helsinki might feel at home with simple modernism. These things have gone deep subject-wise following conditioning. We are all also conditioned to watch much more violent and horrifying movies than people were 100 years ago. The way Western art scenes condition their "inhabitants" to not fear blood, sperm, or piss goes deep.

At the same time, highbrow Western Europeans might have a challenging time watching a goat sacrifice in a small village in the Eurasian mountains – or understanding that in some scenes, breaking boundaries is not just even interesting (in free countries with a liberal culture, like the Nordics).

Strong reactions are, of course, at least one way to know when things go deep and when boundaries (created by conditioning) are strong. But there are also other types of issues. What Heidegger means with the temple is also that it construes a destiny for the inhabitants through its presence, as art's role there is also about questions of destiny like life and death, incorporated into the religious realm of the temple and its impact on everyday life. Sometimes boundaries of this type are made present by an art scene. When artists are taken to court following their deeds, the whole local community has to face the issues. When artist Ulla Karttunen aimed to present at Kluuvi Gallery Helsinki a take on child pornography, just making the point how easy it was to access them, and this became a public issue, people had to face reality to some extent – and the boundaries of what can be accepted. Facing the threat of a jail sentence, the artist forced people to think about the boundaries of what we call freedom and the role of pornography in today's culture. In Helsinki people in the scene really had to face the situation, and even people around it, too. It is not a formally pleasant temple we are talking about here, but a challenge presented by an artwork (that not many people in the end saw) that forced people to take a look at really basic, deep-cutting questions, like how women and even children area sexualized in visual culture.[7] This left traces on everyone in the scene. The scene also found boundaries for what was possible.

Scenes have their constitutive scandals that make scene members, at least the ones with a history there, sensitive to certain issues. Of course, this also happens in whatever organization with a history, but what we are interested in here is the way it affects artistic production, interpretation and experience, too, i.e. what is aesthetic about this kind of an impact. Local ethnic activists, the level of feminism and queer thinking in any scene, or memories of heated debates about artist income and appropriation can fuel and cut many ways of working. Projects evolve or fall following these scandals, and their intellectual echo remains in the scene. People just work and see things differently in different scenes because of these issues. In a city like Tallinn, in the art scene, semiotics is mainstream and philosophy is marginal – the exact opposite of Helsinki, which lies 40 miles away – as Juri Lotman, a major name in semiotics, worked in Estonia, and one can still also see the impact on semiotics on many artworks. Similarly, bringing artworks on tour to different scenes might change greatly the interpretations they face. Here scenes might work in multilateral ways. The main critics with their assumptions about art, the brand of the art museum in the context, and the history of what has been shown make remarkable differences here.

To turn from destinies and groundbreaking questions to more classical questions of aesthetics, another gateway to the topic might be presented by Wittgensteinian aesthetics, for example, Kjell S. Johannesen's and Tore Nordenstam's concept of "aesthetic sensitivity."[8] Johannesen and Nordenstam discuss phenomena like learning the way encounters with art are connected to a sensitivity, something acquired, something we are trained to notice, understand, and enjoy. Harmony in music is a good example, or balance in a picture. These are sensitivities we learn by training. Similar to Frank Sibley's ideas on aesthetic concepts,[9] it probably helps when someone tells us the facts verbally at some point in our development, if we want to be able to use a sensitivity. If no one ever told me when a piece of music or a chord sounded harmonic, could I have ever gained the point of it? Let us think that someone dislikes reggae music but moves to Jamaica, where they will hear it all the time. Slowly they hear differences, like some things and dislike others, and find meanings, aesthetics, and learn a whole sensitivity to the practice – including societal, social, and other (for the aesthetic side) supportive practices around the music. So, to take this to the scenes: we already learned that scenes can have some consistency with Heidegger's fantasies about the Greeks and their temples (his idea that aesthetic objects can have a groundbreaking role in culture is not fantasy, but, of course, he did not know how the Ancient Greeks experienced anything), and that scenes can really constitute something culturally for the people who are in them or just living where the scenes are, but what kind of aesthetic sensitivities could scenes offer that the city around them, and other scenes, do not? This is an easier question to answer. A good take on this could be that you'd think of sound. Some cities have had a music scene that has drifted away from not just the everyday idea of music, but from the way other scenes make sense of sound, too. One can think of, for example, the role Manchester had in the late 1990s and early 2000s. The clubbing, also less uptight than the dominant London clubbing scene at the time, with its new modes of music – from early electro to local rockish music – went beyond classic rock clichés and conventions of sound, sometimes in a way that prepared the audience there to hear things differently, to, phenomenologically speaking, orient themselves intentionally, aesthetically, and artistically to things that might still have appeared somewhere else just as plain noise. In the US, Baltimore and the so-called Baltimore sound had this role in the early 2000s, when catatonic rhythms, together with noises that echoed technical problems, became commonplace. These cities had a music scene that drifted apart from the surrounding scenes and the scenes they were connected to, making new noises and sounds commonplace, educating and conditioning their audience to find, furnish, and foster new sensitivities and sensibilities. This is, of course, something, that on a very small level could happen in the work of one artist (not even connected to any scene), or a small community somewhere (Black Mountain College), but what we are here after is a change in a culture, not a "national culture," nor something that could be all-encompassing for the people in it like the culture of a tribe, but a change which aesthetically makes the aesthetic world, sensibility, sensitivity, and ways of orienting one-self in sound and music different for the people in the sphere in which this happens. We are far from the very conceptual themes of Arthur C. Danto's "Artworld," as the latter is about conceptions of theory and history, not aesthetic sensibility. Making sense of things can change in one place and in a scene, which is more than a community but less than something that we'd traditionally call a culture. In contrast to understanding music in a certain country or region or inside a genre, as the concept is sometimes used (e.g. country music), being in a scene shows us the importance of the intense communication and sensual connection of the people inside the scene of an urban realm.

One could think that some scenes could have deeply and historically local traits that would somehow make sense on a deeper level in their art scenes – like the use of saunas in the Helsinki art scene or the endless intellectual and sometimes even physical brawl between the leftists and the extreme right in Vienna. But a shallow version of Heidegger's thinking could take us to the way some phenomena in the scene take part in constituting the whole, not just in the way that everything is connected to everything, but in a profound way. Think of the way the radical Tokyo art scene of the 1960s (and its "spirit"), where conservative radical writer Yukio Mishima (who committed hara-kiri), butoh dance, blood performances, and ritualistic noise music developed side by side, supporting each other, famously opened a whole new space for thinking, doing, and experiencing. It was a scene where local tradition and contemporary experimentation (Western modernism) took place side by side, a scene that famously also fueled other scenes with its "free and [...] chaotic energy."[10] The Wittgensteinian approach could think that the turns and features of scenes in different cities are a bit more formally and on a slightly more surface level something that one could learn like sensitivity – like taking on reggae in Jamaica after some years. And in a sense, Danto's take on contemporary art is also about deeper level things happening in the artworld, things that make peculiar traits meaningful, that give depth to them – of what goes beyond the visible, what is gained from the context, in Danto's conception of the art system. Of course, some people grow in many scenes – as we have done – and maybe even quite a few people do that. But they do not just learn the logics of the field where they start from the modes of production, economic support, main figures, main sites, and supporting structures like the cafés and clubs, but they learn something else. In some scenes, they learn the invisible, hard-to-catch sensitivities, deep or surface, and variations of the logic of how things happen, and take them with them when they leave their scenes. How much are they portable? This we can no longer ask Duchamp and the French artists who left for New York during the Second World War – and neither can we ask the Jewish composers that escaped the Nazis and settled in Hollywood. We can see forms and practices and artistic styles arriving, but for sure some sort of deeper and more surface sensitivities must have arrived, too, and logics of one scene of the artworld must have entered another.

It is interesting how sometimes scenes have and do not have an impact on the broader whole they are a part of, i.e. a city (or even a small nation). Think, for example, of the incredibly playful and fun design scene of Milan – which was boosted in the late 1960s and thrived throughout the 1970s and 1980s, making the whole city something that we today know partly because of its both cold and playful style, from sunglasses to everyday objects like Minnie Mouse telephones. Its colorful and semi-futuristic take on the everyday through design somehow became commonplace in the city, without forgetting that it had, of course, an impact on other design scenes and everyday life all around the globe. One needs to remind the reader only of the radically beautiful, edgy Olivetti typewriters that Ettore Sottsass designed – we are especially thinking about the *Valentine* model from 1968 – or the happiesque kitschen tools that Matteo Thun made a radical commonplace for the domestic chefs of the middle class. The scene, of course, worked like any scene, being possible and doing well as there was a great designer community working in the city, and as there were potential companies and factories, critics and buyers, for stuff that had to first make it in one place to be taken seriously in another. Collectors finished the process, but the interesting thing is that this defined the life of a whole city aesthetically speaking, the everyday of the snobbish Milanese people, whose relationship to design became a celebrated phenomenon for the whole world.[11]

Speaking in Danto's terms: scenes share an art history – which, of course, has some sort of connection to global or just more close international or national art histories. But they have also their own ethical, sensual, and aesthetic histories. There are also theoretical models of thinking around which affect the way things are done and interpreted in scenes. Scenes are thus small artworlds, connected to a broader network of artworlds. There is, of course, not just one global artworld, but often we interpret it to be that way, to think that mainly things are like this and that, but here it is different. Still, this broader artworld or network of artworlds would probably be discussed very differently in Berlin, New York, and Tokyo.

This takes us, of course, to the hierarchy of scenes, and/or the way there are central and marginal scenes. In central ones, people seem to often have more of a clear idea of universal traits, which we in smaller scenes see through and note as being colonial points of view, where our existence is somewhat overshadowed or dismissed. For some, of course, big scenes also lead – but for many, there is no following, and people from bigger scenes seldom follow what happens in smaller scenes. When you are from Paris, you don't follow Lyon – and from Lyon you don't think you have to go the closest small town to take a look whether there's a scene. You gaze at Paris – or some other center of the world.

It is interestingly so, that scenes are sometimes also trendy – or that they are "interesting" for a while, even if they are marginal. They are suddenly on the map, or then they disappear. Trends build on affordable housing where artists move in. The livable scene takes over. Or trends take over in areas where cities invest in culture, for example, supporting design shops and studios. Cultural production and distribution is governed by national strategies as much as city strategies. These strategies are sometimes just for commerce, or tourism, but often they affect the scene itself. So, big scenes take part in constituting the reality in all scenes, and then, sometimes strongly, local ones, big or small, constitute reality, aesthetic sensitivity.

Discussing scenes could affect even discourse on power relations, post-postcolonialism, and cultural politics. Most of the negative international use of power in culture and the arts does not happen in Riga, Lisbon or Athens – so why talk about Europe, or even more complicatedly the West, when criticizing power-structures? Scenes have a message for postcolonialists, which resembles the age-old instruction that is given to poets: don't say flower if you can say rose – and don't say West or Europe, if everything in the end is about a couple of scenes, like London, Paris, New York, Berlin and maybe, occasionally, in certain contexts, Los Angeles (film), Cologne (sculpture), or Vienna (classical music). Scenes are a more appropriate way to talk about not just the economic issues that run this world's hierarchies and power-relations, as they are culturally central. Classics that we have analyzed in this book show this, from Danto's and Sontag's New York, to the Germans and the French theorists who build discourse on the arts.

Can (Non-) Europeans Think? (2015) – Hamid Dabashi's provocative work on Eurocentric thinking is an example of a book where the West as a concept occupies a major role, although the author discusses actually almost just London, one scene! Looking at this from our perspective, it feels weird, maybe even a little aggressive, to discuss Europe or the whole West, when we are not, for example, in Helsinki or Bratislava, it seems, part of the discussed issue. Dabashi needs to learn that scenes exist – and so do many others.[12] The post-colonialist who attacks big units in the end just adds to the already existing marginalization of the "lesser centers," and still has a long way to go when thinking about power-structures.

We also, of course, have our own experiences from bigger cultural centers – as we have lived or stayed for long periods in Stockholm, Prague, Berlin, Paris, and London, without even mentioning the amount of visits that we have had to make professionally to bigger centers to see the things we desire and need to see. We have come back noticing how many opportunities these places have, and how people in them seem to have a hard time decentralizing themselves, seeing that they are still just in one place, which does not overshadow everything else in this world. But we have, also, seen how many of us, come back from the centers totally colonialized, even brainwashed, thinking that everything that matters is only things that can take place in Paris or New York. These major-scene-philes always connect to the big scene, where they desperately try to still keep one foot, in one way or another, so that they do not lose touch with what "is hip." This form of cultural colonialization and self-colonialization is a sad thing that does not always add to the exchange that scenes could have, as the bigger ones are only occasionally interested in what the smaller ones can offer – and the smaller ones often cannot, of course, really pose anything different for the bigger ones, either. But when they do, they face arrogance and snobbism, as already witnessed in Chapter 1, when we discussed Magritte's career and its relocation from Brussels to Paris.

As there is aesthetics of different arts (dance, comics, painting), and as there is aesthetic research on artistic movements, forms of expression, interpretation, and experience, scenes offer us a frame that goes deep into the aesthetic a priori of some of their "inhabitants," but even more, govern ways of doing things, seeing things, and interpreting, experiencing. There is an aesthetics of the Berlin scene and an aesthetics of the Mumbai scene, and everyone who knows these scenes well understands what that could mean.

When relocating, we take our own scenes to other scenes and add to the multilayer exchange that art scenes have, the kind of invisible networking that glues things together invisibly. Could it be useful to think of scenes through the allegory of wine regions? Most people who do not live in wine regions have the idea that people there taste a lot of different wines, but actually this is not the case often. In the Chianti area people just drink Chianti on an everyday basis. And the wines themselves are, of course, made out of grapes that travel, with methods that are used everywhere, but the wine-drinking people in these areas really get a sort of a touch on the thing through their own area. The mix of grapes, their way of growing in the area, minerals, all the methods of cultivation that certain areas support and reward, and the harvesting methods, together with soil, temperature, local foods (that wines service), and the aspirations of wine cultivators create a unique, but not that different, take on what wines are – and then people in that area drink mostly just that wine, still, of course, understanding other wines, too, through that framework of taste. Still one can have a discourse about wine areas (without them having any of the interpretation or theory-driven effects that Danto focuses on), and what they share. But Malbec is just added to a mix in Bordeaux, while it has raised its own labels and done its own success in some parts of Argentina, where it stands alone as the dominant grape – like contact improvisation in dance staying dominant somewhere, even if somewhere else it is just one thing among others. And Pinot Noir is widely cultivated and used in different ways in Southern Germany, Northern Italy, and California gaining different regional sides into itself. Many go into global matters, trying to taste wines from different areas, and learn about wines more widely, but no one can really know all the wine areas and their differences. And most people, really, enjoy mainly just the wine of their own area – like one enjoys things that are in a way or another provided by one's own art scene, even visiting performances or touring exhibitions through the framework offered by the local mediators, curators, and cultural institutions. And everywhere there are wines that people in other areas really don't know – although they could. In the Chianti area one can have rarely labeled and even nameless wines like Colline di Lucca, which are not sold much elsewhere, but which locally add to the existing realm of wine – like certain choreographers are a local breed that everyone knows in a certain city, and some performers really site-specifically represent just their own scene. And the way one gets trained or the way one tastes things in one region is not that far from the basic idea of how one spends aesthetic quality time in a scene.

Anyway, the immense amount of differences inside of scenes is distracting. For example, professional theaters are in various ways connected to other theaters, both professional and amateur – and through inhabitants of two sub-scenes (film and theater), theaters connect to film, to the extent that one can in some cases see the scene of actors and directors as more dominant than those of film and theater. The same kinds of natural extensions and bridges connect opera and other forms of music, opera and acting, stenographers, sound experts, and various other professional branches. The layers are not only hard to get for external perceivers. Following the more linguistic nature of theater, film, and literature – vis-à-vis visual art and music, these scenes are mostly more geographically restricted to local culture. And the list of possibilities is endless. And all these build us, make some things more natural for us, some sensitivities stronger, and some weaker. There are so many professions where scenes exist, from skateboarding to fashion, and from bio art to rap and poetry, and there are endless cases where one can really ask if it is a scene or not (and people do question it), but the interesting, rewarding, and miraculous thing is the pulse, atmosphere, and culturally constitutive nature of scenes. Being formed and informed by the Norwegian jazz scene or the Baltimore club scene means culturally a lot. It goes beyond practices and conventions, coded traditions and ritual patterns, to the aesthetic a priori.

Kant's originally very fundamental notion concerning perception was already employed by Theodor Adorno and Max Horkheimer in their "Culture Industry" in 1944[13] where the supposed freedom of consumers was debased as a pre-produced set of ways of perceiving and experiencing, an aesthetic a priori hammered with endless repetition of pop music beats, commercial images, and film. And scenes do hammer forms and sensibilities into us.

Like Darwin once speculated on natural selection through ways of adaptation to different environments, it is time for us to think of scenes in the same way – like we have partly been thinking already of cultures like Norwegian or Igbo as building the complex organisms we are. Different types of visual artists survive the competition in Cologne and Riga, very different types of dancers seem to thrive in Helsinki and St. Petersburg (the former being less technical but less constricted by tradition) and those who inhabit the scenes gain their cultural a priori – together with other formative contexts and bases – through living through the stimulation, comforts, and challenges that the scenes provide. Very different types of artists survive the competition in different scenes.

Many questions remain to be asked. When we talk in art history about schools and movements – should we rather talk about scenes? Was Zurich's Dada more of a scene than a movement, or just a community which looked more holistic afterward, as a historical phenomenon? Are some of the historical "schools" and "movements" just scenes that were packaged later on to be schools – like the Prague School of semiotics or the Vienna Circle? What about bohemian circles, where so many artists have been raised intellectually in, for example, Central Europe? The same question haunts schools like Bauhaus and Black Mountain College, or art colonies rules by vegetarianism and/or feminism, without forgetting Paris cubism. All these could be seen at least in some ways possibly not just communities and networks, or parts of the artworld, but maybe, if nothing else, then at least provisionally, maybe as sub-scenes. Scenes, now when really discovered and analyzed, ask for rethinking many issues in cultural studies, art theory and aesthetics. We think the trip has just begun and there is a lot to think about concerning the concept of scenes, but we hope that our book has at least raised the appetite or shown the relevance for future scene studies.

Notes

1 Martin Heidegger, *The Origin of the Work of Art*, in *Off the Beaten Track*, edited and translated by Julian Young and Kenneth Haynes (Cambridge: Cambridge University Press, 2002), 3.
2 Martin Heidegger, *Being and Time* (Oxford: Blackwell, 1962).
3 Martin Heidegger, *Discourse on Thinking* (New York: Harper Torch Books, 1966), 47.
4 Paul Shih-yi Hsiao, "Heidegger and Our Translation of the Tao Te Ching," in *Heidegger and Asian Thought*, edited by Graham Parkes (Hawai'i: University of Honolulu Press, 1987), 93–104.
5 Hubert L. Dreyfus, "Heidegger on the Connection Between Nihilism, Art, Technology, and Politics," in *The Cambridge Companion to Heidegger*, edited by Charles Guignon, 289–316 (Cambridge: Cambridge University Press, 1993).
6 See e.g. Max Ryynänen and Petteri Kummala, "Equipment as Art, Art as Equipment: Notes on Film, Architecture, and Martin Heidegger's Philosophy of Culture," *Contemporary Aesthetics* 21 (2023). https://contempaesthetics.org/2023/03/12/

equipment-as-art-art-as-equipment-notes-on-film-architecture-and-martin-heideggers-philosophy-of-culture/.

7 Annamari Vänskä, "Anatomy of Shock: What Can We Learn from the Virgin-Whore Church?" in *Art, Excess, and Education: Historical and Discursive Contexts* (New York: Palgrave, 2019).

8 See e.g. Kjell S. Johannesen, *Kunst, språk og estetisk praksis* (Uppsala: Uppsala Universitet, 1994).

9 Frank Sibley, "Aesthetic Concepts," *The Philosophical Review* 68, no. 4 (Oct., 1959): 421–450.

10 Kurihara Nanako, "Hijikata Tatsumi: The Words of Butoh," *The Drama Review* 44, no. 1 (T165) (Spring 2000): 17–18.

11 Catharine Rossi's *Crafting Modern Design in Italy: From Post-War to Postmodernism* (London: The Royal College of Art, 2011) gives a good overview of the 1960s trend of using plastic and reactions for and against American kitsch (see, e.g. Chapter 4, "From Mari to Memphis: Processes and Production from Radical Design to Postmodernism," 349–462).

12 Hamid Dabashi, *Can (Non-) Europeans Think?* (Chicago IL: Chicago University Press, 2015).

13 See Theodor Adorno and Max Horkheimer, *Dialectic of Enlightenment (Cultural Memory in he Present)* (Redwood City CA: Stanford University Press, 2002).

Bibliography

Adorno, Theodor, and Max Horkheimer. *Dialectic of Enlightenment.* Translated by Edmund Jephcott. Redwood City CA: Stanford University Press, 2002.

Dabashi, Hamid. *Can (Non-) Europeans Think?* Chicago IL: Chicago University Press, 2015.

Dreyfus, Hubert L. "Heidegger on the Connection between Nihilism, Art, Technology, and Politics." In *The Cambridge Companion to Heidegger*, edited by Charles Guignon, 289–316. Cambridge: Cambridge University Press, 1993.

Heidegger, Martin. *Being and Time.* Translated by John Macquarrie and Edward Robinson. Translated by John M. Anderson and E. Hans Freund. Oxford: Blackwell, 1962.

Heidegger, Martin. *Discourse on Thinking.* Translated by John M. Anderson & E. Hans Freund. New York: Harper Torch Books, 1966.

Heidegger, Martin. *The Origin of the Work of Art*, in *Off the Beaten Track*, edited and translated by Julian Young and Kenneth Haynes. Cambridge: Cambridge University Press, 2002.

Hsiao, Paul Shih-yi. "Heidegger and Our Translation of the Tao Te Ching." In *Heidegger and Asian Thought*, edited by Graham Parkes, 93–104. Hawai'i: University of Honolulu Press, 1987.

Johannesen, Kjell S. *Kunst, språk og estetisk praksis.* Uppsala: Uppsala Universitet, 1994.

Nanako, Kurihara. "Hijikata Tatsumi: The Words of Butoh." *The Drama Review* 44, No. 1 (T165) (Spring 2000): 10–28.

Rossi, Catharine. *Crafting Modern Design in Italy: From Post-War to Postmodernism.* London: The Royal College of Art, 2011.

Ryynänen, Max, and Petteri Kummala. "Equipment as Art, Art as Equipment: Notes on Film, Architecture, and Martin Heidegger's Philosophy of Culture." *Contemporary Aesthetics* 21 (2023). https://contempaesthetics.org/2023/03/12/

equipment-as-art-art-as-equipment-notes-on-film-architecture-and-martin-hei-deggers-philosophy-of-culture/.

Sibley, Frank. "Aesthetic Concepts." *The Philosophical Review* 68, No. 4 (Oct., 1959): 421–450.

Vänskä, Annamari. "Anatomy of Shock: What Can We Learn from the Virgin-Whore Church?" In *Art, Excess, and Education: Historical and Discursive Contexts.* New York: Palgrave, 2019.

6 Film Scenes

Professionals, Institutionally Homeless Filmmakers, and Film Enthusiasts

This book presents various types of careers in various types of art scenes and cultural scenes. It discusses underground and highbrow, regional and central scenes, highlights the nature of scenes all and all, and then different scenes, and their meaning for individual artists (Introduction, Chapters 1–5), without forgetting scholars, as Roman Jakobson's career and role in various 'schools' of semiotics and linguistics shows the importance of intellectual scene builders (Chapter 1). It is hard to understand how scenes work if we do not have detailed accounts on their role in the lives and careers of artists. The careers of Vivien Westwood and René Magritte show what scenes mean for artists on the everyday level (see especially Chapter 1).

As detailed analyses of agents and the structures of scenes, and notes on the history of urban cultural scenes, without forgetting scenes in different cities (Berlin, New York, Tokyo), should have made the point about the importance of understanding cultural scenes, it might be also rewarding to study the way different arts foster different kinds of scenes. At least a sneak peek could provide useful insights. On a small scale, the first five chapters have already, of course, compared music scenes to poetry slam scenes, and fashion scenes to contemporary art scenes, but this chapter, a rather small addition to the whole, is meant to stress the importance of studying how scenes work in different artistic branches, through a sketchy case study.

As the scope of the book does not allow space for many examples, we have chosen film scenes to show, here in the end, how some of the topics already discussed in the earlier chapters find peculiar expressions. Film scenes are extraordinary in the sense that although a city might host no film production at all, film enthusiasts can build a scene with their film clubs. This is never the case with contemporary art, but reading circles can, of course, produce something similar in literature, though nothing comparable to film. The reason might lie in the need to organize a community to be able to show films, e.g. a film club, if one wants to find alternative films for viewing, or just even viewing film in the cinema, which many film enthusiasts consider to be the only real way to watch films.

DOI: 10.4324/9781003412786-7

The scenes of film enthusiasts are not always connected to the professional world of film. If one compares this to contemporary art, where the creators and the audience mix all the time in galleries, the creators always being quite a dominant chunk of the audience too, film looks very much divided, though many filmmakers have a background in film clubs too. We know of several directors who made it by starting in film clubs and working with distribution (sales) – Quentin Tarantino even worked in a video rental store, The Manhattan Beach Video Archives in California (which later moved to Hermosa Beach),[1] and many of the French new wave directors were really famously active film club members; the same goes for Aki Kaurismäki.[2] Film clubs and associations where film is at the center are very educational communities.

Ted Cohen states that just as there are some films which we consider to be highbrow and others which have a more mainstream or even B-film reputation, there are also audiences, which could be labeled high and low.[3] Cohen's case is for the 'bilaterality' of film, i.e. the way Alfred Hitchcock's films can be watched both by film club enthusiasts, some of them very elitist, and the everyday viewer who grabs a beer and plops on the couch after a long day at work.[4] This is a special feature of film scenes, one that could never exist in poetry or contemporary visual art. Theater, on the other hand, might share this essential divide, as another grand audience art, at least to some extent – but there the highbrow and the lowbrow audiences see different plays. Both arts have once been and are still in certain countries and scenes major forms of public and popular culture. With film it is ironical that film studies became a legitimate academic practice after the height of the importance of cinemas in Western culture (they are still important in e.g. India), "at a time when film is threatened to be superseded by the so-called new-media," as Anton Kaes wrote in 1995.[5] At the same time this decrease of the centrality of cinema culture also made film clubs more important, and film viewing in cinemas increasingly scene-driven practice.

One typical scene profession where enthusiasts who are still a part of the audience only can easily drift into is criticism. Many *auteurs* of film, again one can mention many from Jean-Luc Godard to Aki Kaurismäki,[6] started their professional life in film as critics – bridging their cineaste lives to make a dime, only to then make movies.

Film scenes, like other scenes, have their professional hierarchies. While (mostly male) directors carry with them the echoes of early modern ideas of artistic genius,[7] the costume department, gendered (female), is expected, often without institutional support, to take home the dirty textiles and wash them on their free time.[8] Film people note that while art museums often show the work of female artists, the film industry is very much male-driven. As a result, associations like Women in Film have become important for the profession.[9]

In terms of education, film scenes often resemble literature scenes, where writers can be educated, but in many instances, they aren't educated and they are even proud of this (famous cases being beatniks and other underground poets in literature). While painting, when studied, is about modern and/or contemporary art, and there isn't really a scene for non-educated painters (if marketplace art/kitsch is not counted in), film often has people working on its highest Pantheon who have little or no film education. This is the case with again, in reference to my own scene; Aki Kaurismäki, studied communications[10] but he is not alone. Other famous film makers who did not study film include, e.g. Ava Duvernay, Wes Anderson, Stanley Kubrick, Christopher Nolan, James Cameron, Peter Jackson, Tim Burton, Quentin Tarantino, and Ethan Cohen. Thinking about the quintessential role of these names in what we think of as feature film today, it is remarkable how film can still live in this kind of situation. It also tells something about the shallow role of film schools in the scene. If art schools are pretty much everything for the base of contemporary art scenes, film schools are not that fundamental for film scenes. Exceptions exist, of course, like the role of the Academy of Performing Art in Prague (Forman, Kusturica, etc.). (In smaller towns, art schools, of course, have a more central role – even in film.) Of course, it is also a well-known fact that in pop music people don't often come from music schools, but also there the education system is not as developed as it is for film. The world is full of even national film schools, which one cannot say about schools of rock and pop music.

After gaining their diploma in film, even educated film makers end up working for TV, more broadly the moving image and/or commercial audio-visual culture (e.g. doing promo videos) and using their knowledge to run festivals and film companies. As we have been teaching (besides film programs) in various programs which are interdisciplinary, there have been many film makers who have 'fled' the film scene and the more official, or legitimate profession of film making, citing the many institutional problems. One of these problems is, of course, the central role that the film world (together with popular music) had in the #MeToo phenomenon, but others relate to the tough work that dealing with commercial cinema craves, not just artistic work nor the long hours, but the heavy extra work on production and the many logistical issues (often also a problem in TV production), which can make artistic work sometimes feel marginal in the whole.[11]

Another interesting thing is that while literature is still what it is as a profession, and literary scenes have counted as they have pretty much been for ages,[12] the audiovisual culture has recently grown into a major form of expression with Instagram videos and the moving image on the internet and on smart phones (the amount of non-educated everyday film makers increasing), together with the expansion of the role of the moving image in contemporary art, where one can already talk about 'gallery and museum film,' which is a whole sub-scene of contemporary art today with its films which can be viewed nearly only in galleries, biennials, art halls and museums, and which has already its own stars, like Eija-Liisa Ahtila, Mariko Mori and Paul McCarthy. Their rise has to do with the way the tech used for film making became very much cheaper in the late nineteenth century (this development has continued). As a result, there are various ways in which film makers, after concluding their studies in film, if they have any, can build their professional agencies today.

First and foremost, film scenes are more divided into makers and enthusiasts, but they also feature more people escaping the scene (no one escapes the poetry scene for its bad atmosphere or gender problems) as already noted above. Another interesting peculiarity is the broad and rich professional community that film is. With every feature film there are people who work with the audio, the scenography, acting, even catering and other issues. The crews are probably the largest and most varied in their professional expertise than in any other art (sub) scene. Every scene has people who are also in other scenes, but in film, the number of them who are often best paid in the movie scene (writing for movies is better than poetry, and film music pays better than jazz), is greater than in others.

At the same time, the film world is heavily concentrated on 'national cinemas.'[13] National might not always be a good word to use for most arts and the lives in their scenes (as we have shown in this book), such as contemporary art scenes and music scenes which are often more centered around cities (Stockholm and Malmö for Sweden, Copenhagen for Denmark, etc.). Film production, on the other hand, has reasons to be viewed through the national perspective (even if the film industry is very much often situated in capital cities, at least in smaller countries), partly based on the need for economic support, which in many countries comes through national broadcasting television and national film funds. For example, Henry Bacon discusses the breakdown of the studio system in Finland as a properly national enterprise that was lost, and which lowered film production in Finland for decades, even leading some directors to rediscover their professional identity in other countries,[14] and this huge dependence of film on studios, funding, cinemas, TV, and many other large institutions defines its scene, which is always also about money, bigger than in most other arts, with the exception of popular music. At the same time, following film's inescapably national nature, transnational filmmaking networks, like Kurdish minority film, have issues with registering their films nationally.[15] Within the European union, producers are also forced to work for international co-productions because of the funding from Eurimages (European cinema support fund).

Focusing on just the film studios and their role, Kimmo Laine neatly packages some of that scene-wise in his introduction to *Finnish Film Studios* (2022), by stating without hesitation that the scene has been ideologically national for a long time and then even economically, through subsidies starting from the 1960s – and by accentuating that "Finnish feature film production has been really dominated by a few major studios."[16] The book also shows how models were taken not from Hollywood, but from the experiences in other scenes, like the film production world of Sweden, a neighboring country that is larger, more prosperous, and more famous in film.[17] Equipment, caterers, hang-around patrons, carpenters, and costume departments,[18] inspiring and dominating studio moguls (as Laine has it) and office workers make studios not only places to work and meet, but platforms for things to happen and to be tested, professionally or more narrowly aesthetically. While Hollywood studios might have dominated the world, but ultimately acted as institutional agents in the film world of Los Angeles, in smaller countries the effect of studios remains quite local.

The rise and fall of studios affect minor as well as major film scenes. For example, it is a well-known fact that the destruction of Cinecittà in (the bombing of) Rome (by Western Allies) had a drastic effect on film making in Rome, and was one of the leading reasons for the way the neorealists began open air filming.[19] Studios, have been the places that bring film people together. Douglas Gomery's great *The Hollywood Studio System: A History* describes how the big studios, with their early age, film-crazed producers, managed to create whole worlds, with settings used in countless films, enormous crews, their own restaurants and cafes, and building communities as if they were giant circuses or small villages.[20] In the case of the major studios, one can even ask if they stand for a whole scene of their own!

Talking about film scenes, it is mostly not like in poetry, where film makers would hang out in the same café – a historical element that also applies to the lives of painters. They could have done that, but this is not an issue in film history. For film scenes, coming together has traditionally been more driven by professional platforms, studios at the center, and, of course, the already mentioned film clubs and other platforms of cineastes being fertile ground for slowly growing into film making. As most of the studies in this book show, regarding the interconnectedness of looser platforms of meeting people, from cafes to openings, film, as any other art, has its own rituals, including premieres and festivals, where people come together.

Still today, as experienced teachers in art universities, we can say that while contemporary artists, the ones we teach, often end up running what they call 'spaces', not just galleries, but places where things happen through talks and seminars and screenings too, film students end up having their own production companies or running small festivals. Their networks grow mostly more 'national,' and, thinking about, e.g. contemporary artists (and the ones who do moving image in the 'art scene'), less transnational.

After an entire book of takes on geographically different scenes, and notes on the differences between different kinds of art scenes, this small sketchy take on film scenes only is just one beginning in the project of starting to study comparatively the way art scenes work, and on the way to realizing the potentials of scene thinking and the benefits of a higher understanding of scenes. We hope that this scratch will foster new takes on different arts, including deeper insights into how film scenes work and how they differ from other artistic scenes.

Notes

1 Hilary De Vries, "Cover Story: A Chat with Mr. Mayhem," *Los Angeles Times*, September 11, 1994. https://www.latimes.com/archives/la-xpm-1994-09-11-ca-37458-story.html.

2 Peter von Bagh describes Kaurismäki's university years in Tampere as being a life of someone crazy about film, a cinefile – accentuating Kaurismäki's way of watching movies and being present (also in the Finnish film archives, where von Bagh curated film series). Peter von Bagh, *Aki Kaurismäki* (Helsinki: WSOY, 2006), 8.

3 Ted Cohen, "High and Low Art, and High and Low Audiences," *The Journal of Aesthetics and Art Criticism* 57, no. 2 (1993): 137–143.

4 This does not mean that film clubs would consist of highbrow viewers only, but the tenet of watching films definitely owes more to the highbrow tradition in all of them e.g. through concentration on the material, thinking about life works of directors, and other features typical for the art system. On these traits, see e.g. Ryynänen, *On the Philosophy of Central European Art*, especially Chapter 1.

5 Anton Kaes, "German Cultural History and the Study of Film: The Theses and a Postscript," *New German Critique* 65 (Spring-Summer 1995). Quoted in Anu Koivunen and Astrid Söderbergh Widding, eds. *Cinema Studies Into Visual Theory* (Turku: University of Turku, School of Art, Literature, and Music, Series A, 1998), 13.

6 von Bagh, *Aki Kaurismäki*, 9. On the New Wave, see e.g. Richard Neupert, *A History of the French New Wave Cinema* (Madison: University of Wisconsin Press, 2007).

7 For more on this, see e.g. Larry Shiner, *The Invention of Art: A Cultural History* (Chicago IL: University of Chicago Press, 2001). See also Christine Battersby, *Gender and Genius: Towards a Feminist Aesthetics* (London: The Women's Press, 1989).

8 Danai Anagnostou, "To Address Femininity Via Studying Below-The-Line Film Labour Practices," *Popular Inquiry* 5, no. 2 (2019): 53–59.

9 See the webpages of this international association: https://womeninfilm.org.

10 Kaurismäki actually applied to film school, but wasn't accepted. Peter von Bagh, *Aki Kaurismäki*, 8, 17.

11 See e.g. the research results on the webpages of the European Women's Audiovisual Network, EWA: https://www.ewawomen.com/research. See also e.g. Neil Percival, "Gendered Reasons for Leaving a Career in the UK TV Industry," *Media, Culture & Society* 42, no. 3 (2019): 414–430; Shirley Dex and Richard Paterson, "Freelance Workers and Contract Uncertainty: The Effects of Contractual Changes in the Television Industry," *Work, Employment and Society* 14, no. 2 (2000): 283–305. One of my favorite film directors in Finland, Janne Kuusi, quit the work following the multitasking and the heavy production processes. See e.g. Katja Incoronato, "Elokuvien teon jättänyt ohjaaja," *Uusi Suomi* 25.3.2018. https://www.uusisuomi.fi/uutiset/elokuvien-teon-jattanyt-ohjaaja-surkeissa-olosuhteissa-synnytetaan-monen-laisia-haitallisia-tyotapoja/09050e4a-9bbd-3eb1-a8e2-161d8973bfb3.

12 One can of course think that changes like fan fiction, audio books, or the economic challenges in the publishing system could be remarkable for the profession and its economy, but in the end they do not affect what we have in this book discussed as scenes.

13 For an overview, see e.g. Valentina Vitali and Paul Willemen, eds., *Theorizing National Cinema* (London: British Film Institute, 2006). See also Graeme Turner, *Film as Social Practice* (London and New York: Routledge, 1988), 134–146.

14 Henry Bacon, "Nordic Practices and Nordic Sensibilities in Finnish-Swedish Co-Productions: The case of Klaus Härö and Jarkko T. Laine," *Journal of Scandinavian Cinema* 4, no. 2 (June 2014): 99–115. For a historical view on the studio system, see also Kimmo Laine, *Finnish Film Studios* (Edinburgh: Edinburgh University Press, 2022).

15 See e.g. Özgür Çiçek, "The Fictive Archive: Kurdish Filmmaking in Turkey," *Alphaville: Journal of Film and Screen Media* 1 (Summer 2011): 1–18.

16 Kimmo Laine, *Finnish Film Studios*, 14–15.

17 Ibid., 71.

18 Ibid., 15.

19 There were of course also aesthetic reasons for choosing the streets for the studios at the time, but one cannot overview that the studio suddenly was mostly not a possibility for filmmakers at the time of this change. For a brief historical survey of these historical changes, see Noa Steimatsky, "The Cinecittà Refugee Camp (1944–1950)," *Postwar Italian Cinema: New Studies* 128 (Spring 2009): 23–50.

20 Douglas Gomery, *The Hollywood Studio System: A History* (London: British Film Institute, 2005).

Bibliography

Anagnostou, Danai. "To Address Femininity Via Studying Below-The-Line Film Labour Practices." *Popular Inquiry* 5, No. 2 (2019): 53–59.

Bacon, Henry. "Nordic Practices and Nordic Sensibilities in Finnish-Swedish Co-Productions: The Case of Klaus Härö and Jarkko T. Laine." *Journal of Scandinavian Cinema* 4, No. 2 (June 2014): 99–115.

Battersby, Christine. *Gender and Genius: Towards a Feminist Aesthetics.* London: The Women's Press, 1989.

Çiçek, Özgür. "The Fictive Archive: Kurdish Filmmaking in Turkey." *Alphaville: Journal of Film and Screen Media* 1 (Summer 2011): 1–18.

Cohen, Ted. "High and Low Art, and High and Low Audiences." *The Journal of Aesthetics and Art Criticism* 57, No. 2 (1993): 137–143.

De Vries, Hilary. "Cover Story: A Chat with Mr. Mayhem." *Los Angeles Times.* September 11, 1994. https://www.latimes.com/archives/la-xpm-1994-09-11-ca-37458-story.html.

Dex, Shirley, and Richard Paterson. "Freelance Workers and Contract Uncertainty: The Effects of Contractual Changes in the Television Industry." *Work, Employment and Society* 14, No. 2 (2000): 283–305.

Gomery, Douglas. *The Hollywood Studio System: A History.* London: British Film Institute, 2005.

Koivunen, Anu, and Astrid Söderbergh Widding, eds., *Cinema Studies Into Visual Theory.* Turku: University of Turku, School of Art, Literature, and Music, Series A, 1998.

Laine, Kimmo. *Finnish Film Studios.* Edinburgh: Edinburgh University Press, 2022.

Neupert, Richard. *A History of the French New Wave Cinema.* Madison: University of Wisconsin Press, 2007.

Percival, Neil. "Gendered Reasons for Leaving a Career in the UK TV Industry." *Media, Culture & Society* 42, No. 3 (2019): 414–430.

Ryynänen, Max. *On the Philosophy of Central European Art: The History of an Institution and Its Global Competitors.* Lanham MD: Lexington Books, 2020.

Shiner, Larry. *The Invention of Art: A Cultural History.* Chicago IL: University of Chicago Press, 2001.

Steimatsky, Noa. "The Cinecittà Refugee Camp (1944–1950)." *Postwar Italian Cinema: New Studies* 128 (Spring 2009): 23–50.

Turner, Graeme. *Film as Social Practice.* London and New York: Routledge, 1988.

Vitali, Valentina, and Paul Willemen, eds., *Theorizing National Cinema.* London: British Film Institute, 2006.

von Bagh, Peter. *Aki Kaurismäki.* Helsinki: WSOY, 2006.

Index

Note: Page numbers followed by "n" denote endnotes

For Product Safety Concerns and Information please contact our EU
representative GPSR@taylorandfrancis.com
Taylor & Francis Verlag GmbH, Kaufingerstraße 24, 80331 München, Germany

www.ingramcontent.com/pod-product-compliance
Lightning Source LLC
Chambersburg PA
CBHW050539270326
41926CB00015B/3297